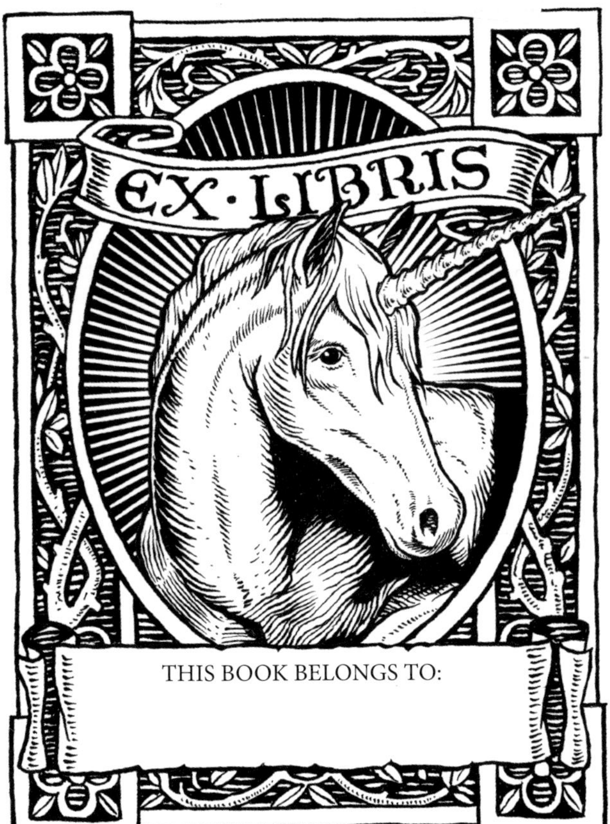
EX·LIBRIS
THIS BOOK BELONGS TO:

Unicorns

by

Anne Stokes

and

John Woodward

Published in 2018 by Anne Stokes Collection Limited

www.annestokes.com

Second Edition

Text by John Woodward. Paintings by Anne Stokes.
Sketches and line art by Anne Stokes and John Woodward.

Distributed by Eastgate Resource Limited
www.eastgateresource.co.uk
Printed in the UK

ISBN 978-0-9569446-4-1

CONTENTS

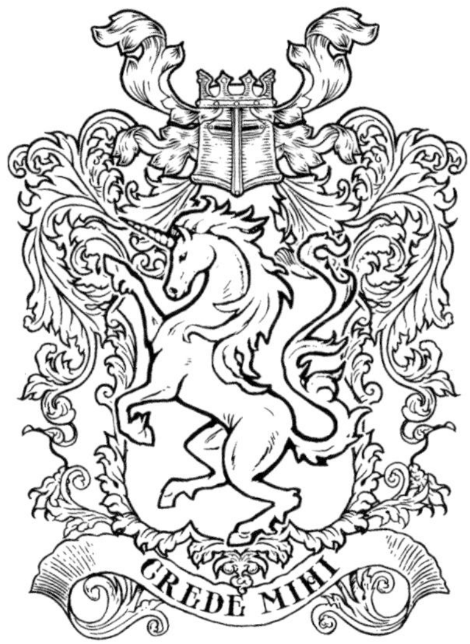

Solace

Unrequited love is a terrible burden for the heart and none should ever feel the loneliness it creates. She thought that by running until she could run no more it would abate, just enough to find solace. But alas, it only took her further into a world she did not know and become truly lost. In that instance her heart cried out a beseeching plea and was answered most unexpectedly.

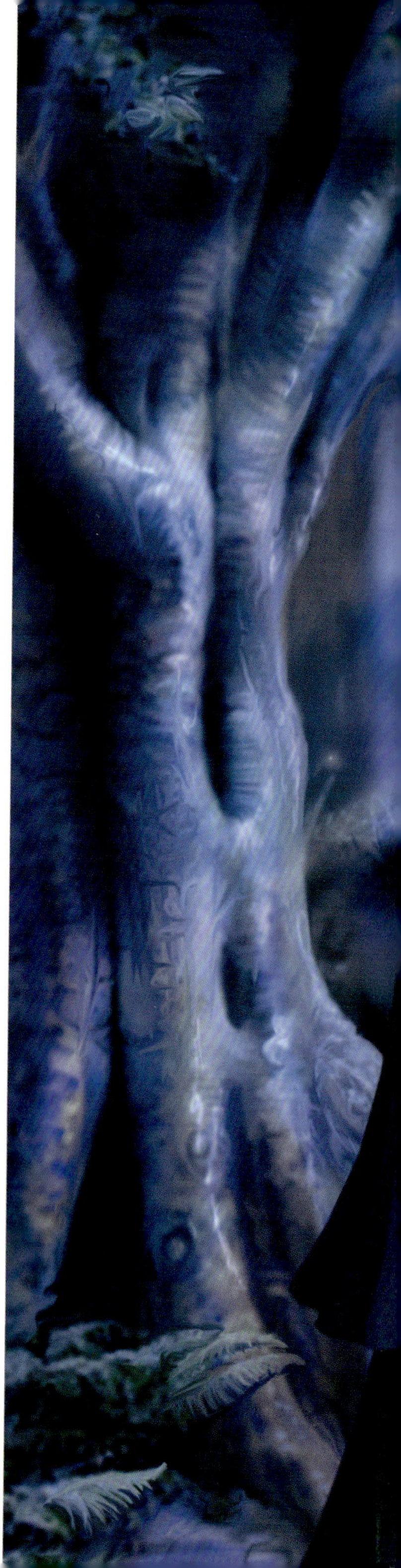

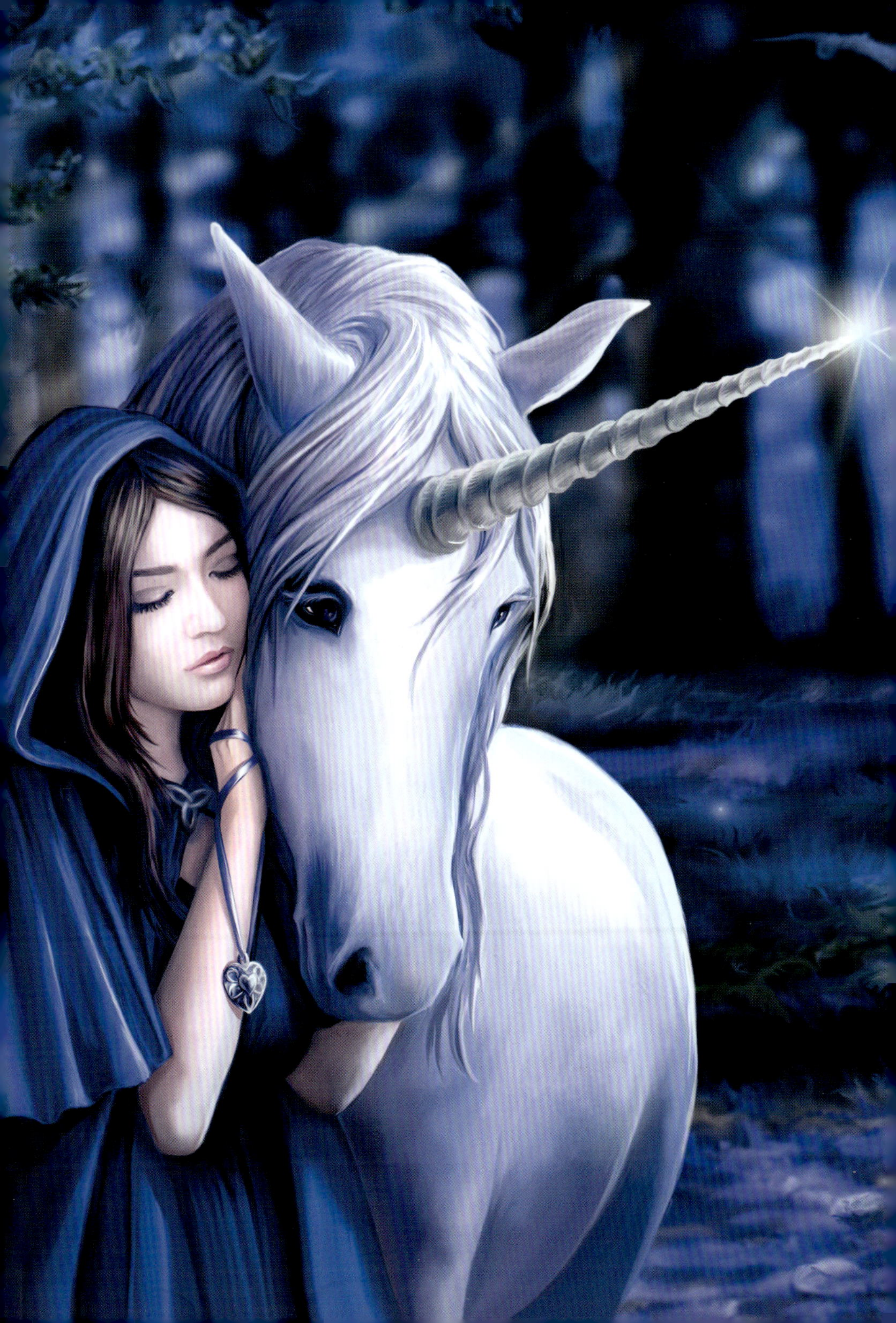

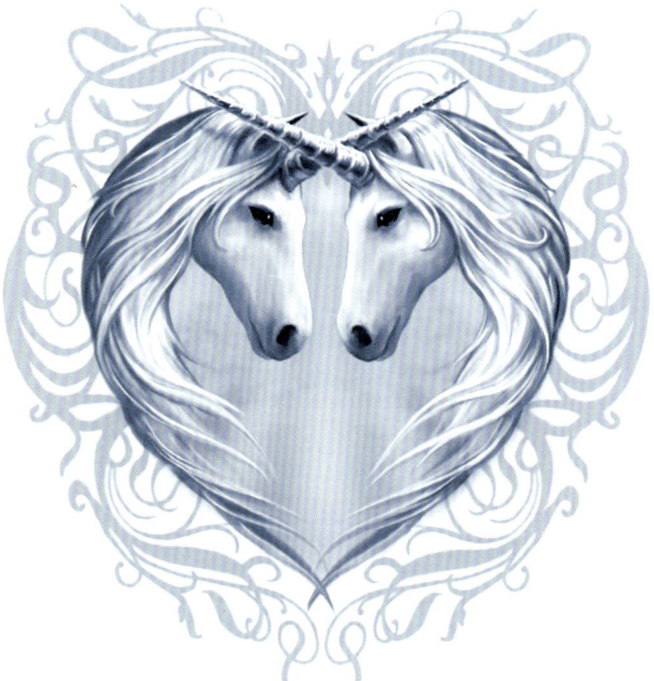

Introduction

Within this book, internationally renowned fantasy artist Anne Stokes and author John Woodward take you on a journey into the world of the magical and elusive unicorn.

For hundreds of years, the unicorn has become synonymous with mystery, blessings and hope. Surely whenever we think of this beautiful creature we feel an inner sense of joy and peace. Why exactly is that? What is the history behind this most curious of beasts?

Anne's paintings continue the legacy in depicting the beautiful unicorn, allowing us to embrace its enduring appeal. No gentle and magical creature has held a fascination more.

Delve into the enchanting history that has captured our hearts and minds for over two thousand years.

"Earliest known accounts of its existence date back to pre-civilization..."

CHAPTER I

History

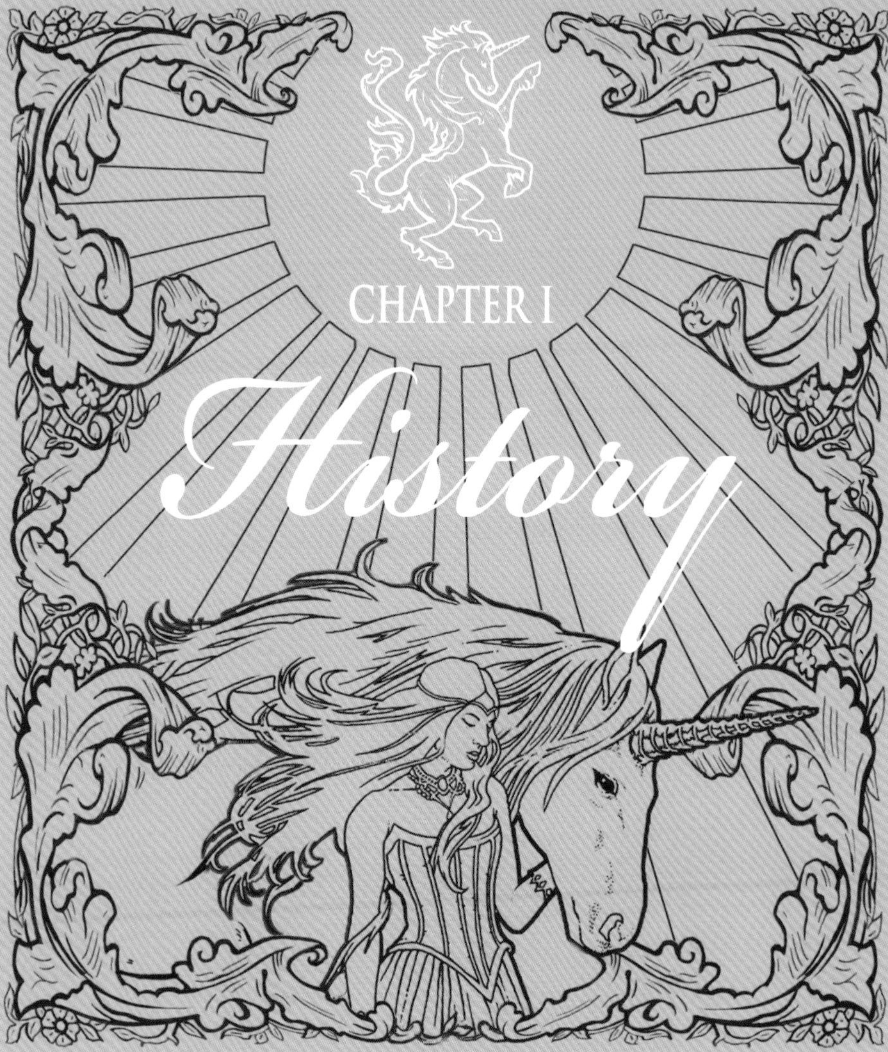

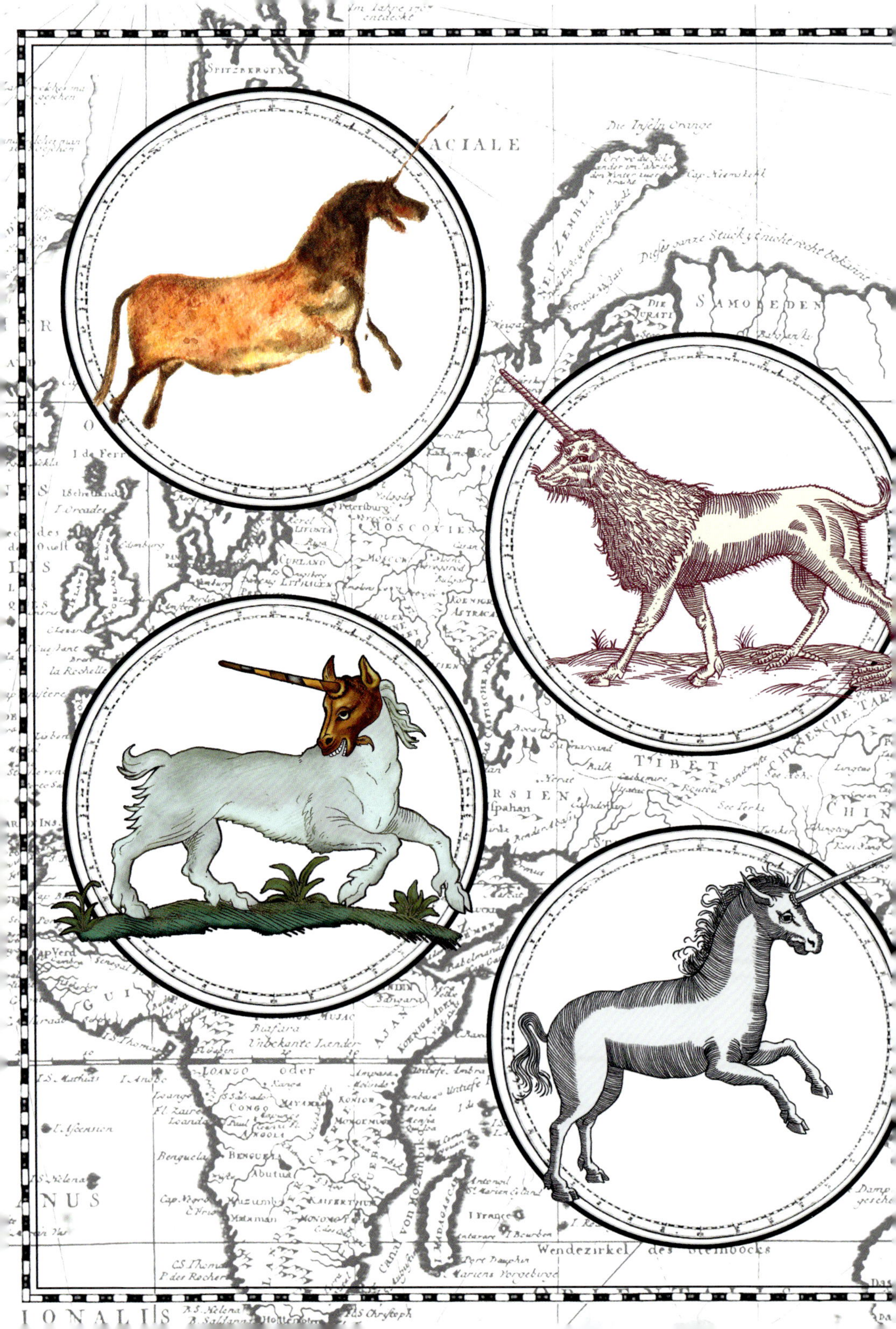
SPITZBERGEN
Die Inseln Orange
NEU ZEMBLA
Petersburg
CURLAND
LITHAUEN
la Rochelle
TIBET
Ispahan
Cap Verd
LOANGO oder
Biafara
Unbekante Lender
CONGO
BENGUELA
Benguela
Abutua
I. Ascension
S. Helena
I. France
I. Bourbon
Wendezirkel des Steinbocks

The journey from the earliest depictions of one-horned-beasts to the rainbow-fluffy-incarnation we know today is indeed a long and fascinating one. Throughout history and from countless civilizations around the world are accounts of the unicorn. Though strong and proud, it is also noble and kind. While many mythical creatures denote danger, the unicorn is an omen of good luck and seen as a constant light in the eternal darkness. In art, sculpture, literature and entertainment it has remained at the heart of mythology right up to present day.

Earliest known accounts of its existence date back to pre-civilization. Depictions of a single-horned beast are found in Palaeolithic cave paintings at Lascaux cave, near the village of Montignac, France. Discovered in 1940, it is estimated that they are up to 20,000 years old and some of the finest examples of early man's cave art ever found. One of the animals has been dubbed 'The Unicorn', and for a very good reason. It stands out from the rest as it doesn't look like any real animals of the region at that time. Some experts believe that it may be a human in an animal costume, possibly to get closer to other animals during the hunt or indeed maybe a representation of a mythical creature. Personally, I subscribe to the latter theory.

Although never featured in Greek mythology, ancient scholars actually believed that this creature was real. It was thought that it made its home in India, a magical and mysterious distant land to them at the time.

They are mentioned in early writings on the subject of natural history. Innumerable writers of that age including the Greek physician Ctesias of Cnidus, Pliny the Younger wrote about them. **Claudius Aelianus** (175-235 AD) in his collection *'On the Nature of Animals'* written around 230AD wrote *"In India there are wild asses as large as horses, or even larger. Their body is white, their head dark red, their eyes bluish, and they have a horn in their forehead about a cubit in length. The lower part of the horn, for about two palms distance from the forehead, is quite white, the middle is black, the upper part, which terminates in a point, is a very flaming red".*

However it is not only in Europe are there documented reports of unicorns but in many cultures and civilizations throughout the world.

The famed warlord **Genghis Khan** (1162-1227) decided not to conquer India after meeting a unicorn, which allegedly bowed down to him; he viewed it as a sign from his dead father and made his formidable army turnaround and return home.

It is said that **Alexander the Great** (356-323BC) was once gifted with a unicorn by Queen Candace of the Ethiopians as a tribute.

In the 7thCentury, the noted scholar **Isidore of Seville** (560-636) stated in a treaty on natural history, that the unicorn *"is very strong and pierces anything it attacks. It fights with elephants and kills them by wounding them in the belly."* He also helped to popularize the myth that would serve as a hallmark in European folklore for centuries to come: That catching a unicorn is impossible...unless it is lured by a virgin woman.

In his travels, **Marco Polo** (1254-1324) believed that he had stumbled across the fabled unicorn. In the account of the meeting he wrote, *"They are very ugly brutes to look at. They are not at all such as we describe unicorns."* Which was unfortunate, as we know today, he was actually writing about the rhinoceros.

Even the illustrious **Julius Caesar** (100-44 B.C.) is recorded as documenting an encounter with a one horned animal whilst in the Hercynian Forest in Germany during his conquest of Gaul.

The **Sanctae Peregrinationes**, published in 1486, was the world's first printed illustrated travel-book; it describes a pilgrimage to Jerusalem and the things seen and encountered upon the way. It featured many large woodcuts, mostly detailed and accurate views of cities. The book also contained pictures of many animals seen on the journey, including a crocodile, camel and of course, a unicorn.

Here are some other interesting variations on the unicorn myth from around the world:

Originally native to southern India, the ***Yale*** or ***Yali*** was somewhat of a contradiction in terms in that it was a unicorn with two horns.

Moreover, unlike the fixed horn of the true unicorn, the double horns of the ***Yale*** could be rotated in different directions, enabling it to aim them at any attacker approaching from any direction. The size of a horse, it sported the tusks of a boar, the tail of an elephant, and the spots of a leopard. Not surprisingly, this startling beast was reputedly kept inside Indian temples to ward off evil spirits.

In Chinese and other East Asian cultures there is the ***Qilin*** or ***Kiri,*** a mythical hooved chimerical creature, it is said to appear with the imminent arrival of a royal baby or the passing of an illustrious ruler. Its image is a good omen thought to occasion prosperity or serenity. As well as its horn it is often depicted with fire all over its body.

In Japan, the ***Kirin*** has the body of a bull and a shaggy mane and was feared, especially by lawbreakers, as it was able to detect guilt. Judges would consult with the ***Kirin*** to determine the guilty parties in legal disputes.

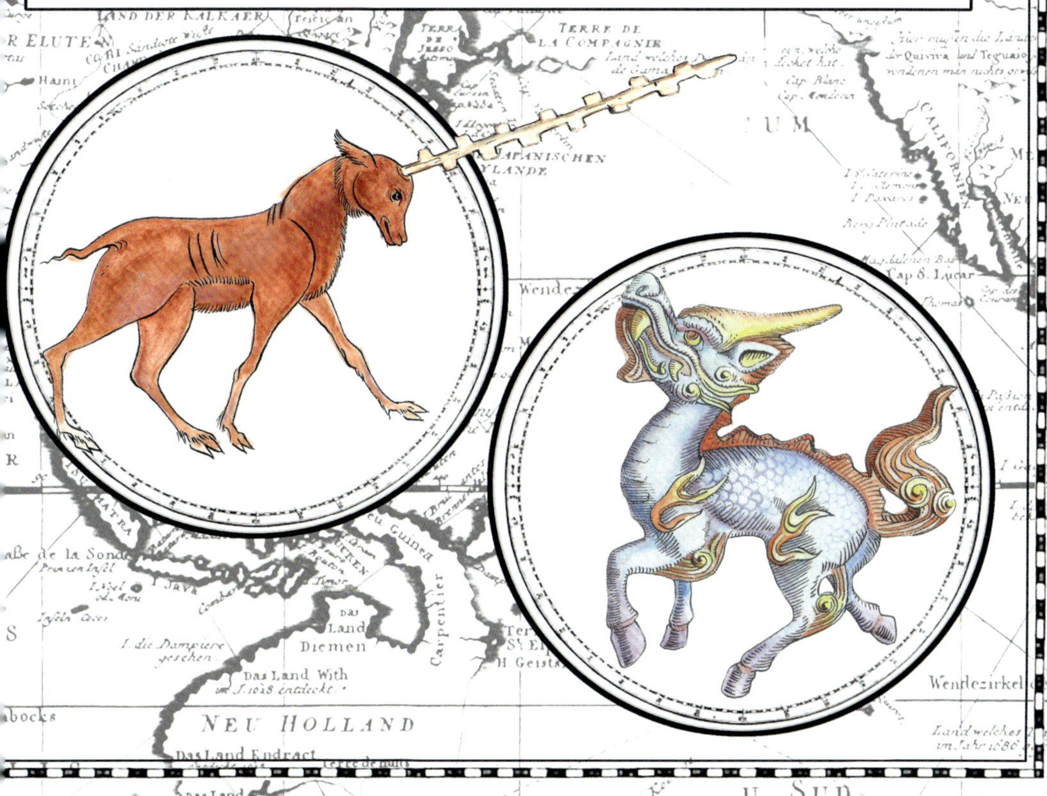

This seems to be a constant in the unicorn myth, of it having the power to divine truth. It is written that it would pierce the heart of a liar with its horn upon meeting.

The ***Karkadann*** is a mythical creature said to live on the grassy plains of India and Persia. The word *kargadan* coincidentally means rhinoceros in Persian and Arabic.

The ***Shadhavar*** - this charming and gentle creature is known from the Medieval Muslim zoological literature, and in the writings of Muslim scholars such as al-Qazwini or al-Damiri. It has one horn with 42 hollow branches and when the wind passes through them, it produces a pleasant sound that makes all animals sit around and listen.

In Russian folklore, the ***Indrik-Beast*** is a fabulous beast and the king of all the animals, who lives on a mountain known as 'The Holy Mountain', when it stirs, the world is said to tremble.

From Chilean mythology the ***Camahueto*** is a mysterious sea-creature that has the form of a calf or bull with a single horn on its forehead. It is born deep within the earth and as soon as it emerges makes its way to the sea to live the rest of its life.

Scotland too has a legend of a Unicorn like creature; it's called the ***Baiste-na-scoghaigh*** of Skye. A shape-shifting creature confined to the Isle of Skye in Scotland's Inner Hebrides. The ***Baiste*** can assume the appearance of a unicorn at will. Additionally, the ***Baiste*** can take on the form of any humanoid whose heart it has eaten. It is related to the ***Bicorne*** (a mythical creature with demonic undertones).

In 1612 **Petrus Plancius** (1552-1622) included a unicorn constellation, Monoceros, on his celestial globe, enshrining the magical beast a place forever in the stars. It is located on the celestial equator between Prion and Hydra.

A Christian metaphor regarding the unicorn is made in the text of **Physiologus** (a 14th Century form of Christian instructional manual using animals, birds and fantastic creatures as allegories). Here to the cleansing power of its horn at a large lake where animals congregate to drink: *'But before they are gathered, the snake comes and throws his poison in the water. So many animals notice the poison and dare not to drink, and they expect the unicorn. It comes and it goes immediately to the lake, with its horn making the sign of the cross, it makes the poison harmless. All other animals drink then'.* Symbolically, the snake that poisons the water is the devil and the unicorn represents Christ the redeemer.

No text from antiquity could be more influential in keeping the great myth of the unicorn alive than the Bible, or to be precise, its insertion into the Hebrew Bible. The ***re'em*** is an animal mentioned several times and is variously translated as unicorn, often as a metaphor representing strength.

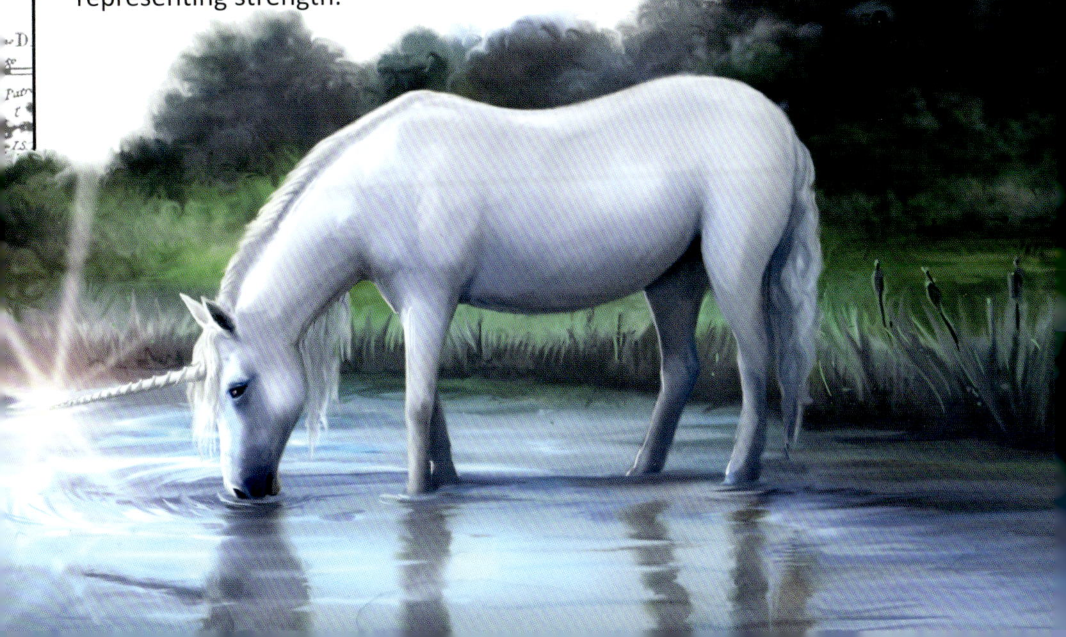

The King James Version of the Old Testament also used unicorn to translate ***re'em***, thereby providing a recognizable animal that was known for its un-tameable nature.

"God brought them out of Egypt; he hath as it were the strength of a unicorn." Numbers 23:22

"His glory is like the firstling of his bullock, and his horns are like the horns of unicorns: with them he shall push the people together to the ends of the earth." Deuteronomy 33:17

"Save me from the lion's mouth; for thou hast heard me from the horns of unicorns." Psalms 22:21

"But my horn shalt thou exalt like the horn of the unicorn: I shall be anointed with fresh oil." Psalms 92:10

"And the unicorns shall come down with them, and the bullocks with the bulls; and their land shall be soaked with blood, and their dust made fat with fatness." Isaiah 34:7

"Will the unicorn be willing to serve thee, or abide by thy crib? Canst thou bind the unicorn with band in the furrow?" Job 39:9–11

Christian monks around the 13th Century wrote several animal fables concerning Noah's Ark which involved wholly mythical beasts. According to one fable, the unicorns did not make it onto the ark because they were too busy laughing and playing to give heed to Noah's warning about the ensuing flood. As an allegory I suppose it is similar to Aesop's 'The Ant and the Grasshopper'. In that one may drift through life and make no preparation for the hardships that will inevitably come along.

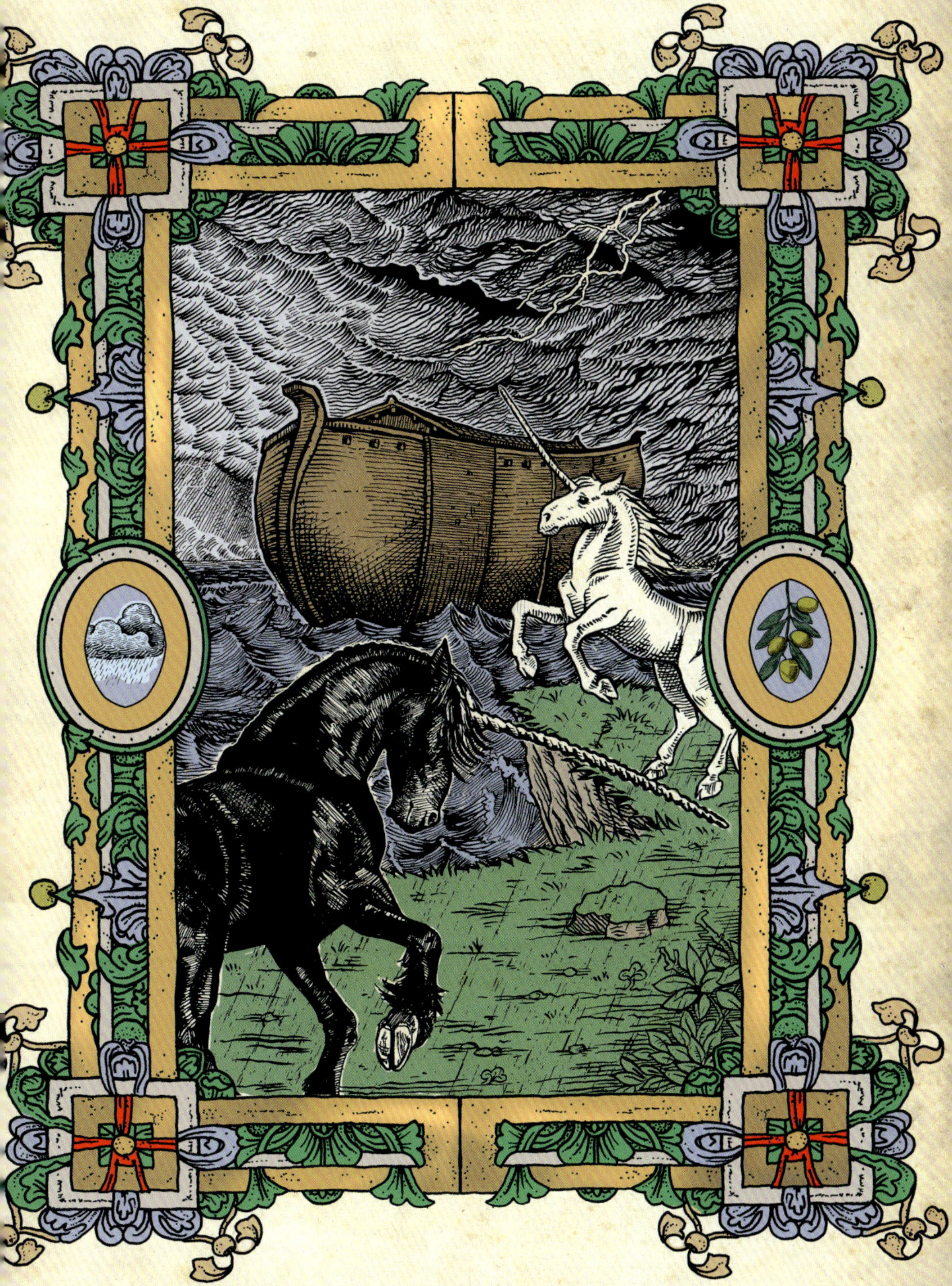

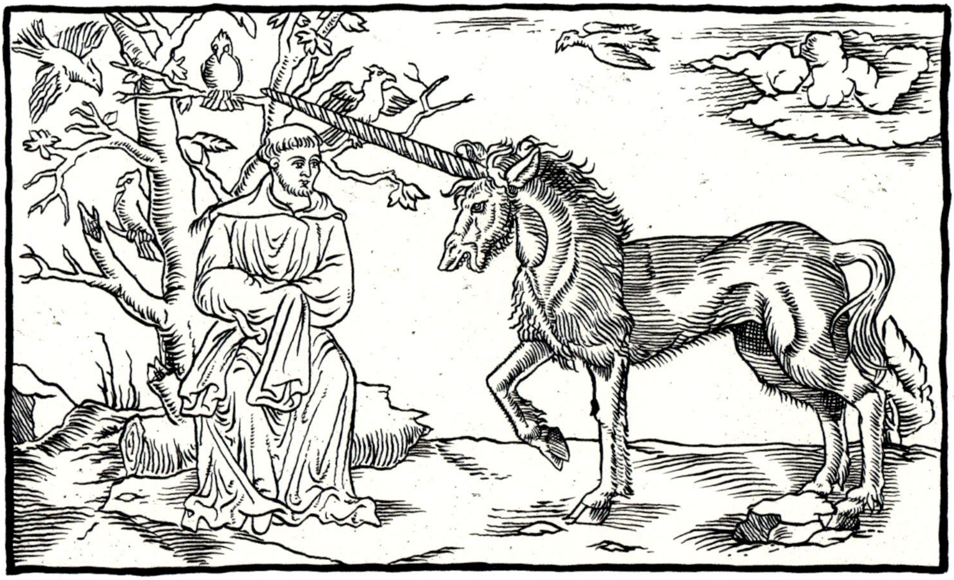

The Monk and the Unicorn

Story by John Woodward

Legend has it that in the early part of the 8th Century in the monastery of Lindisfarne, off the northeast coast of England there lived a young monk by the name of Brendan. It is told that with a simple brush, made of willow and badger fur, he could illustrate biblical text so beautifully that would make an angel shed tears of joy.

Life was far from easy in that isolated place. The constant winds that came in off the North Sea chilled the body to the bone and if provisions were needed, then the nearest settlement was at Lowich, an eight mile arduous walk away. It was a journey that Brendan would always volunteer for, as it afforded him the opportunity to visit the forest at Dean Burn. Here, he would seek out earthy deposits of yellow and red ochre, elderberries, blue berries and even malachite from within a cave he'd discovered. These and other finds were the raw materials he would use in making the colours needed for his illustrations. He thought it the most magical place he knew.

And so it was, on a fine early morning in May he left the monastery with nary a look back. The sun that had risen had the promise of being bright and warm and Brendan hailed it and smiling walked merrily along. By the time he had reached the edges of the forest the sun was high in a clear blue sky. The cool waters from the brook quenched his thirst and he looked for a spot in which he could rest and eat. He came upon a small circular clearing with a large stone at its exact centre. It appealed to Brendan immediately and he clambered onto the rock and made himself comfortable. As he ate his makeshift meal of dark bread and cheese curd he had the strongest feeling of being under observation. Yet there was no one to be seen. Suddenly the hair rose upon his neck and arms and he swung around to look directly behind him, it took him several moments to realise what he saw. A unicorn looked back at him with pale blue eyes almost quizzically. Brendan slid from the rock very slowly, adjusting his body to his gaze and stood there speechless.

How long he stood there he could not tell for time seemed to literally stand still and both never left the gaze of the other. Finally he gathered himself together and modestly bowed. The unicorn in response gave an imperceptible nod, turned and walked away and slowly was lost from sight in the surrounding foliage. Brendan's eyes stayed upon the last space the unicorn had occupied and although his face was expressionless his mind was in turmoil. Was it really a unicorn he had just seen? Was this some sort of jest by forces unknown? Or was it simply that his mind was finally lost to the ravages of the hours spent at his work? His legs gave way and he slumped to the floor in a most undignified manner, and as he lay on his back looking up into the azure sky he paid no attention to the swifts darting hither and thither above. Finally he let out a peel of laughter of such sheer joy that echoed out through the trees. Deep in the forest the unicorn halted and pricked an ear, she heard the laughter and understood its meaning and her heart soared.

As the year progressed and the seasons changed Brendan made the journey as often as he could. The Abbott commented several times that he sincerely hoped Brendan was not shirking his duty to God? Although he knew it not to be true, for of late Brendan's work had taken on a new depth of devotion. His illustrations exuded life even richer than before.

All subsequent journeys had resulted in a meeting with the unicorn. At each meeting he would talk for hours about this or that and the unicorn seemed to listen attentively. He clownishly would impersonate the way Abbot walked with a waddling motion (due to his love of mead, it was rumoured) and chuckled to himself. At the last reunion, he had approached warily and gently caressed its head and ran his fingers through its mane, all the while reciting soft words of comfort. Indeed if it can be said, at that last parting, the unicorn looked sad and Brendan was unaware of the tear that was shed for him as he turned and walked away.

The sky that morning in December was as black as pitch as he set off from the monastery. Snow had started to fall with the first light of dawn, gently at first, and then heavier as he approached the forest. Now that the branches were bare the woods had a feeling of desolation which made him feel melancholic. A sudden distant wolf cry brought him from his reverie and made Brendan aware of his vulnerability.

It had long ceased to be about the resources he found within that place and purely about meeting the unicorn and to be in its presence. Through the falling snow he could make out the stone, which in summer was at the centre of the clearing. It was in that moment he became aware of the weather, which had now grown into a severe blizzard around him. Another wolf cry, followed by another and then another, he knew he must find shelter and quickly, but where? Instantly he thought of the cave.

He made to move in that direction, when from nowhere, sprang the largest wolf onto the stone. Its eyes were fixed unwaveringly onto him and its mouth curled into a snarl from which came a threatening growl. Brendan made to step backwards, until a growl behind him made him turn his head slowly. Sure enough there was another wolf to his left and one directly behind him. He sensed the other to his right. He brought his head to look directly at the pack-leader upon the stone. At that moment the wolf leapt.

Brendan lay dying. He knew that death was near and he also knew that he would greet him as an old friend. He was now in his eighty-seventh year and he had led a good life. Indeed, was he not Bishop of Lindisfarne and in his time so many opportune changes he had brought to this and many other places of worship? He allowed himself a smile; mistaking this act for one of pain, a young monk came to his side to see if he needed succour. Brendan kindly waved the boy away. A breeze blew the white muslin that covered the window and it billowed softly into the chamber.

In that moment he clearly remembered how large the wolf was as it leapt at him, jaws open wide. Then he was knocked into the snow as from seemingly nowhere came the unicorn. The wolf was intercepted from its prey and found itself reeling sideways from the blow against the interloper's hard body. The other three rushed in, the one to the rear of the unicorn received a kick to the head and it turned and ran whimpering from the scene. Without pause the unicorn brought up its front leg and caught the wolf to its left under the jaw with such force that it turned completely over and landed hard into the snow. It quickly righted itself and ran away not daring a glance back. The alpha male sprang to his feet and snarled up, as did its remaining companion to the unicorn that had moved position to shield the fallen Brendan. Both wolves advanced. At that moment the unicorn raised its head high in a majestic movement and a light so pure and radiant burst forth from its horn with such blinding intensity that the darkness of the weather was vanquished. Both wolves yelped and ran off in opposite directions.

Silence descended and the unicorn leant and nudged at Brendan, who raised an arm and stroked its neck gently. He shakily rose to his feet. Using the creature as support they had both slowly made their way to the edge of the forest in the direction of the monastery. There they had parted, yet, not before Brendan took the unicorns head in his hands and touching his forehead to its nose said simply, "Thank you".

He'd returned to the forest several times after that but he never saw the unicorn again. In time he threw himself wholly into his work distracted by nought and continued to illustrate scripture as if touched by God himself.

Now it was time and he closed his eyes one last time.

At that exact moment, in a forest not far away a tear ran down a unicorn's cheek for the second time only.

The End

Moonlight Unicorn

Amidst the ruins of man's undoing, the waters lap against the shore. The moon in full is revealed by parting clouds whose beams highlight the bleak terrain. In that moment a sparkling apparition takes form out of the mist and darts to the lake's edge. Reflected in its eye the melancholy for a landscape long since past, and its tear falls to make the water a little deeper than the night before. Only the shifting ominous cloud dispels the haunting.

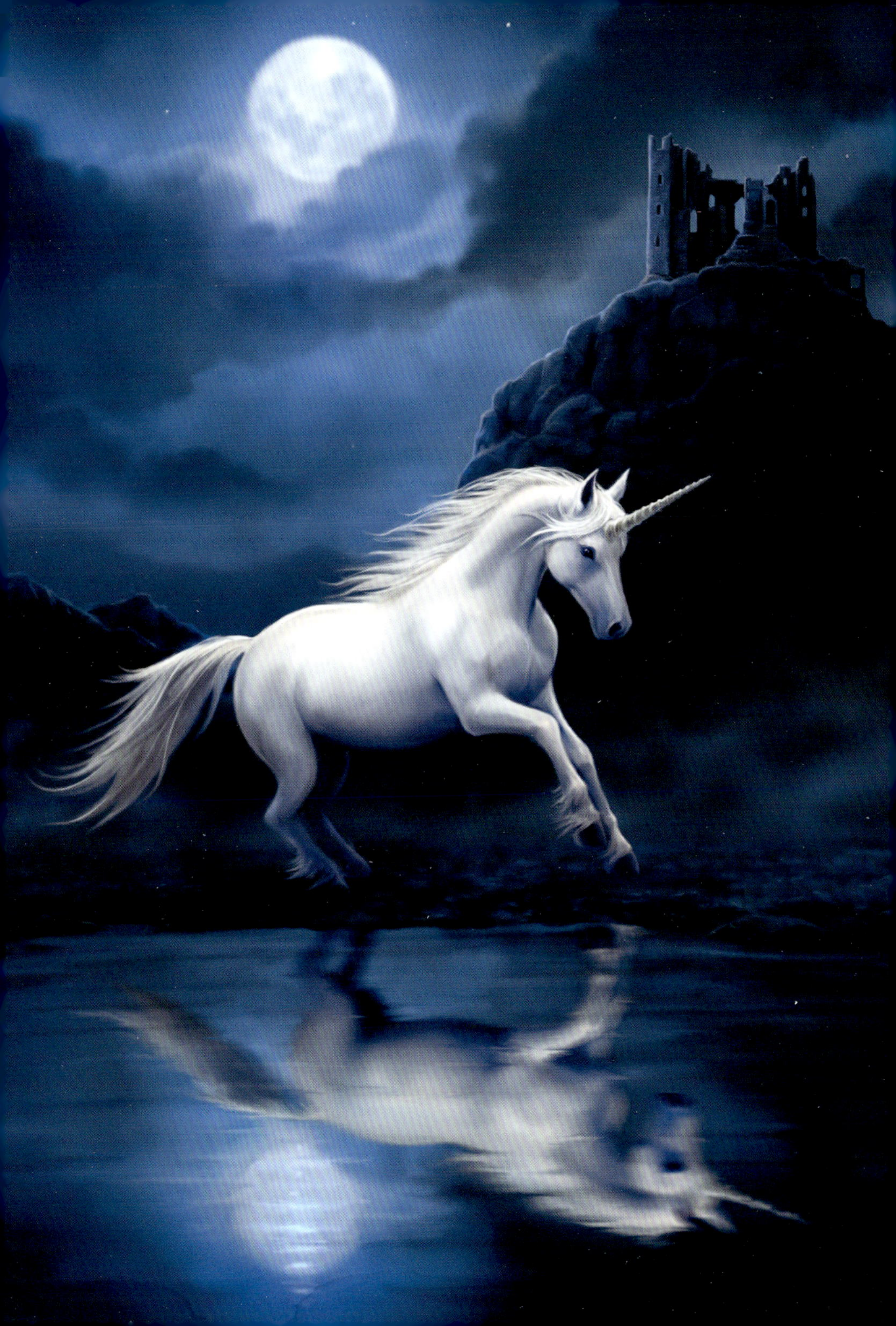

"...the unicorn was the most recognizable symbol of an apothecary..."

CHAPTER II
Unicorn Horn

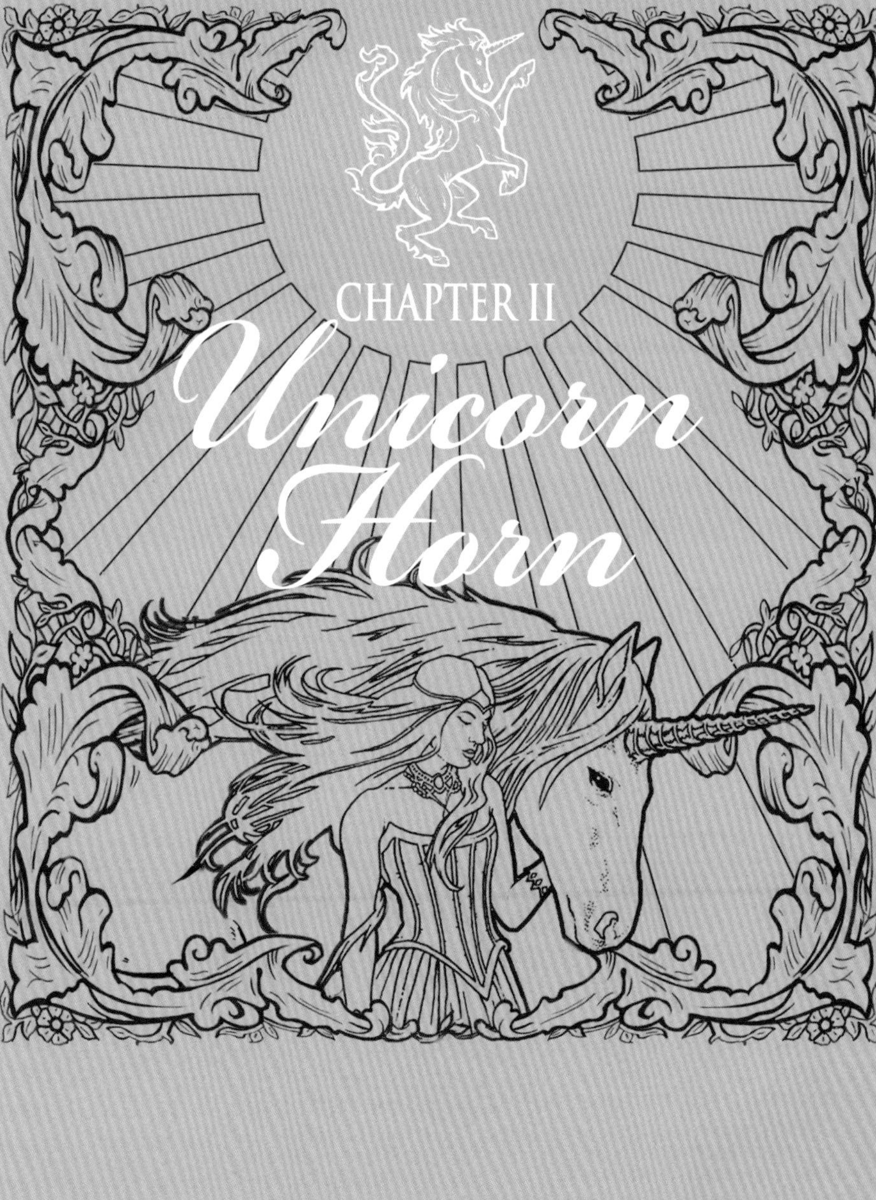

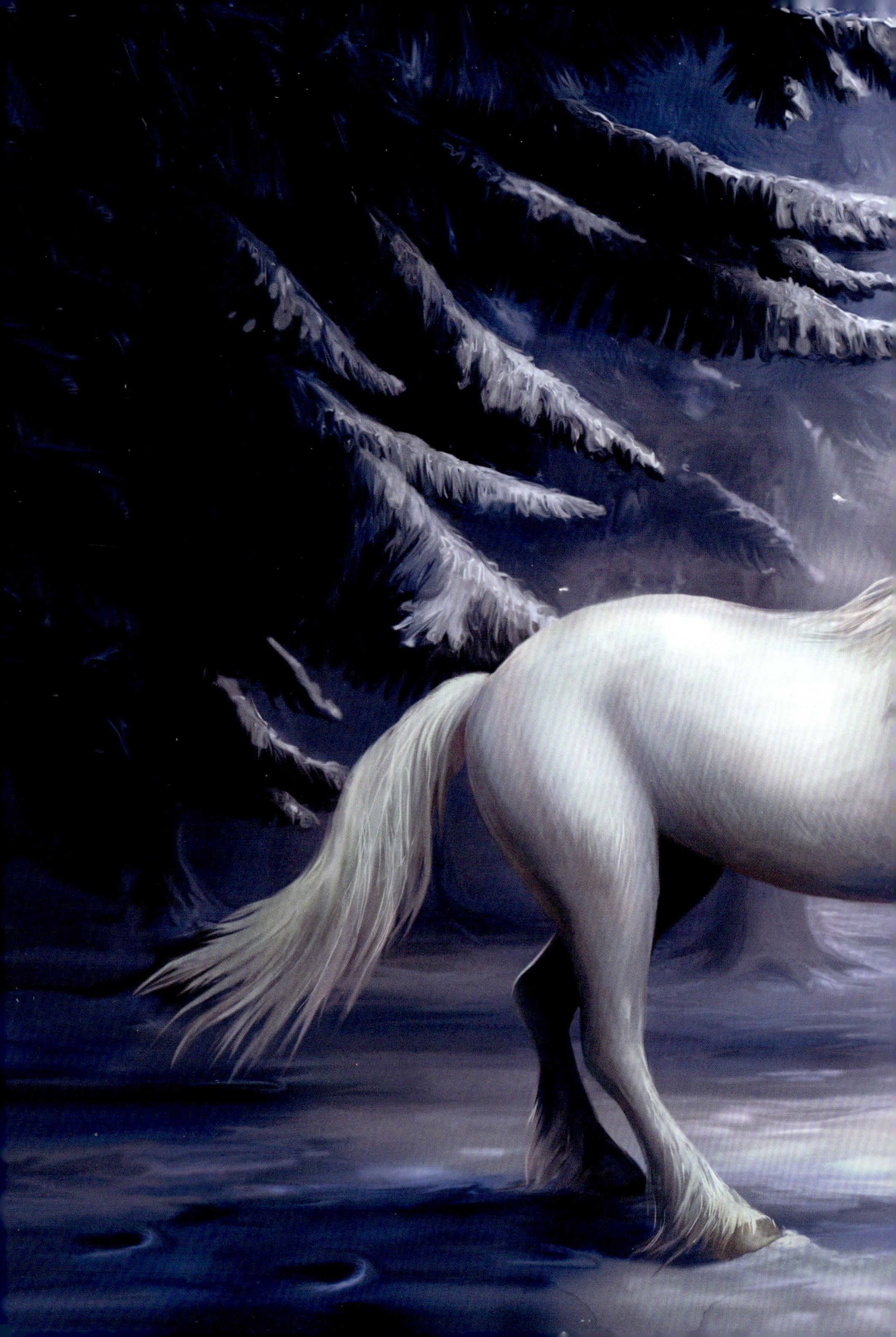

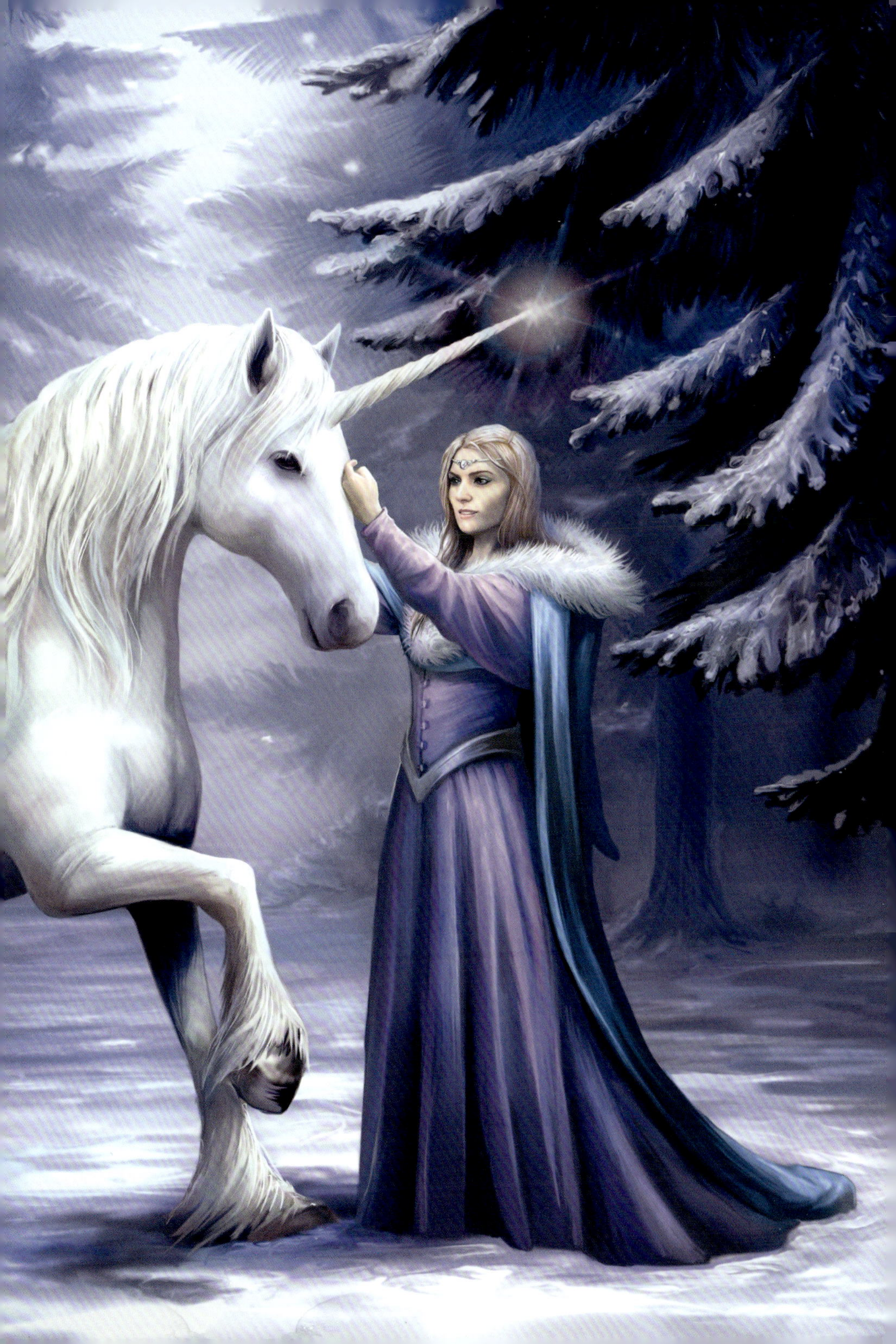

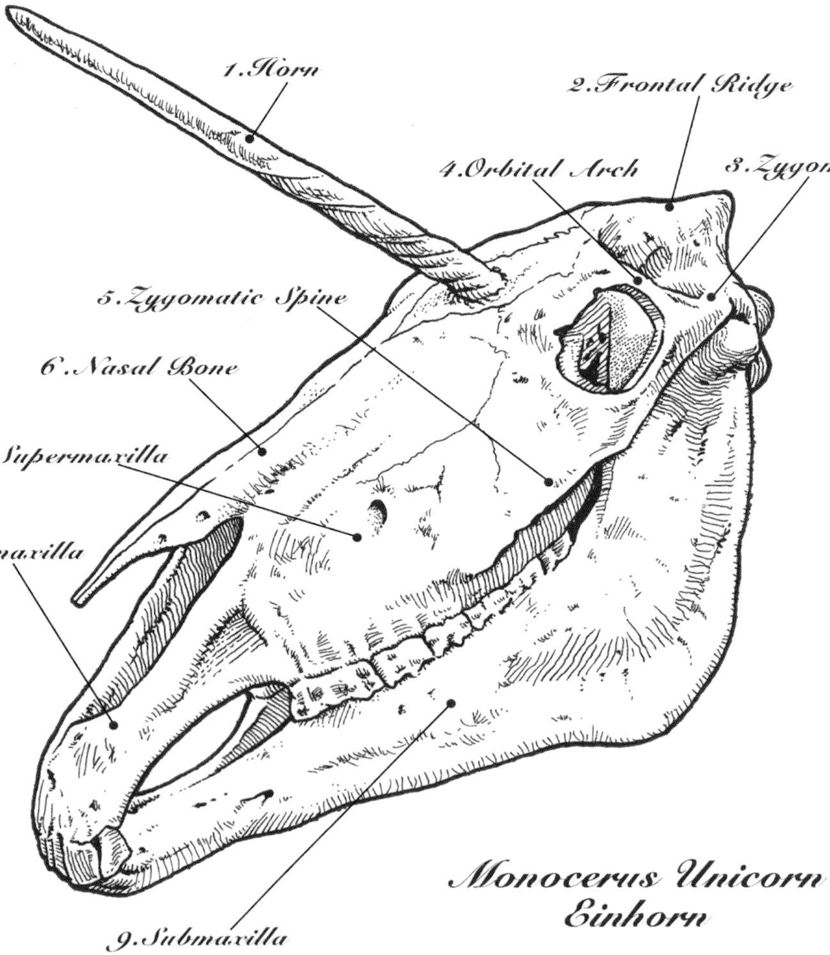

Monocerus Unicorn
Einhorn

It is without a doubt that the most distinctive feature of the unicorn is the horn that spirals from its forehead. As we saw earlier, the shape and length has varied and yet its singularity is the whole cause of its history and fascination. Therefore, due to the important role as a treasured and magical item we shall dedicate this chapter entirely to it.

The horn of a unicorn is called an ***alicorn.***

It is interesting to note that it is only by the Middle Ages that the unicorn had become depicted as a horse or goat like animal. Very much the image we know today rather than the previous varied incarnations. From the 13th - 16th centuries artists began to endow the unicorn with a beauty to befit his noble role as an allegory of so many virtuous attributes i.e. wisdom, purity, magical and Christian. Predominately white in colour and with a long luxuriant flowing mane, cloven hooves and in some instances, with a goat-like beard.

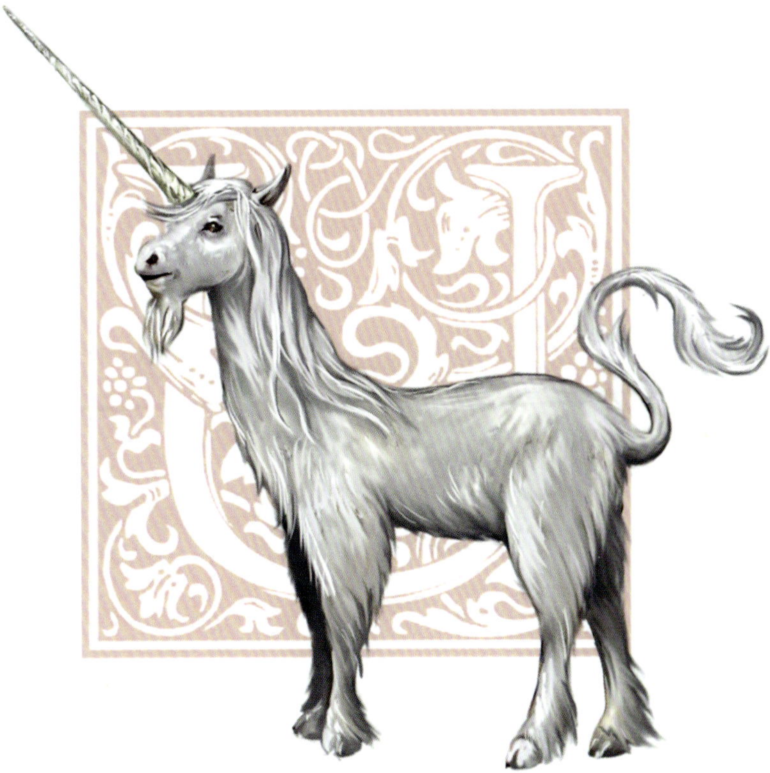

The spiralling of the horn in its portrayal is most likely the result of the introduction into general society of Narwhal tusks, culled by sailors and sold as unicorn horn. These horns were believed to hold magic powers, such as neutralising poison, curing melancholia, convulsions, epilepsy and many more ailments of the time. During the Middle Ages it is recorded that the Parisian monasteries of Germain-des-Prés and the Abbey of Sainte-Geneviève, both used to soak unicorn horn in the drinking water and give it to lepers and other poor unfortunates encumbered by various diseases of the times. It was a very lucrative time for Vikings and other northern traders who were able to sell them for many times their weight in gold. They of course never revealed their true source, the poor over hunted Narwhal.

Not just the horn was believed to be the source of magical properties. In Wolfram von Eschenbach's 13th Century Holy Grail Romance, Parzival (in English, Arthurian knight Percival); the healing element is described as a jewel that is to be found at the base of the unicorn's alicorn.

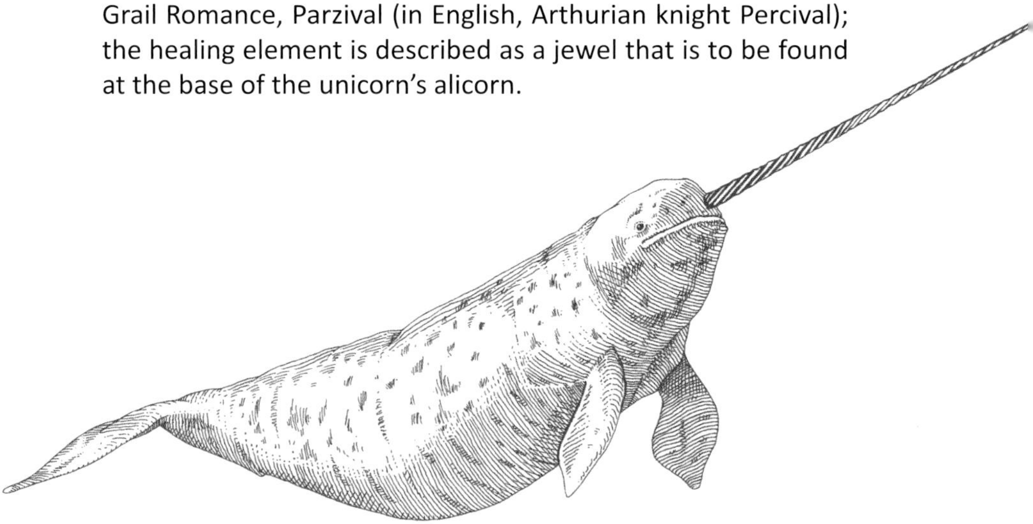

A curious fact is that the narwhal horn is not a horn at all, but a tooth. Comparable to the tusks of elephants or warthogs, but there the comparison ends as it doesn't have a hint of a curve to it.

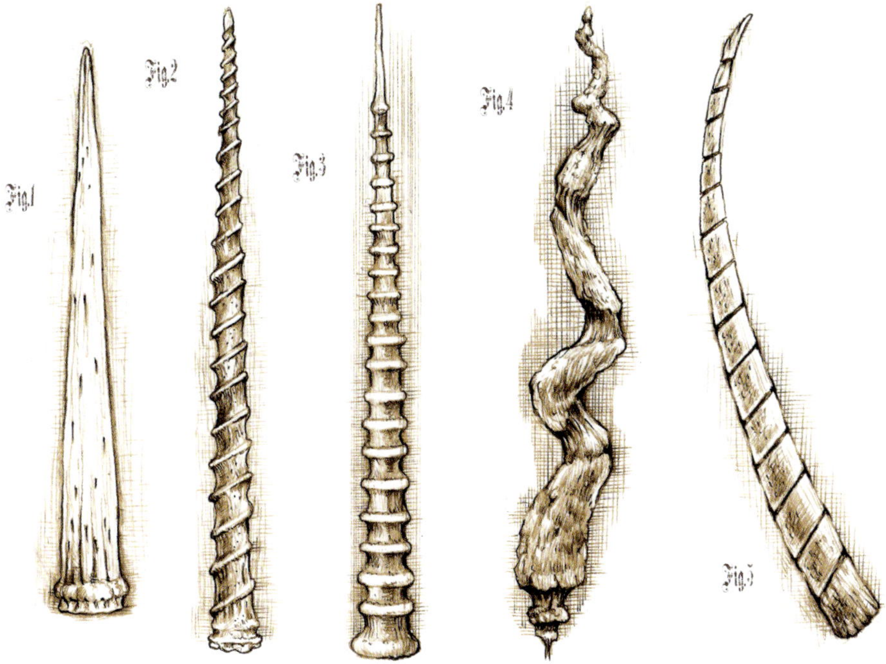

By the Renaissance its miraculous properties had grown so much that it was also believed to sweat in the presence of poison, thereby making it a very handy poison-detector. Presumably something that anyone of importance would require during this dark period of history? Many works and treaties are devoted to the explanation and defence of the medicinal properties of the unicorn horn. The most notable include 'The Treaty of the Unicorn; Its wonderful properties and its use', printed in 1573 by the philosopher Andrea Bacci (1524-1600) and 'Natural History, Hunting, Virtues, and Use of Lycorn', from 1624 by apothecary Laurent Catelan (1568-1647). Bacci, it is theorised, wrote his book at the request of his patients, who were major investors in the unicorn horn trade.

A startling fact concerning the use of unicorn horn related to medicine is documented from the 16th Century. Around this time physicians had very few instruments and objects at their disposal. Yet they were very pious as well as considering themselves as would-be-scientists. As such what they did have and use in their practice were considered to be instruments of

God. The Inquisition played a role in this belief: to doubt the powers of the horn meant doubting the existence of the unicorn itself, an animal of God which was clearly mentioned in the Bible. Therein, to be sceptical of its powers meant the risk of being burned alive at the stake.

It was also one of the most valuable assets that royalty could possess. The Unicorn Sceptre is part of the Austrian Crown Jewels which reside at the Schatzkammer, Vienna, Austria. Early records state that the shaft of the present sceptre was turned from the legendary horn of a unicorn. In reality however, as we know now, it is made from the tusk of a narwhal. The Sceptre bears the signature of Andreas Osenbruck, goldsmith to the Emperor Matthias and was commissioned around 1612, who was crowned King of Bohemia the year previously.

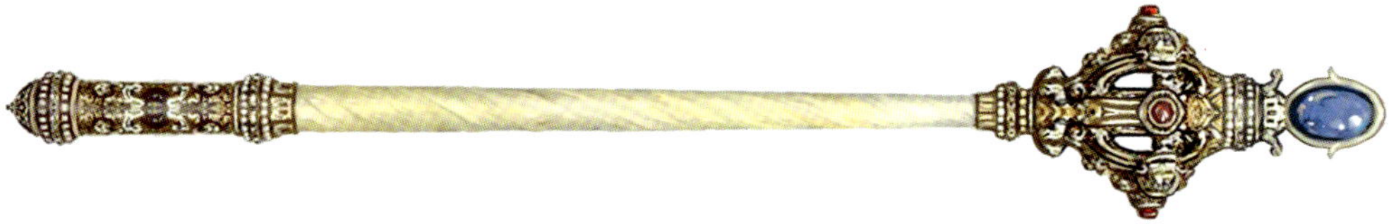

Queen Elizabeth I of England (1533-1603) was the proud owner of two specimens of unicorn horn. The first was kept in her cabinet of curiosities, reportedly paying £10,000 for it, which was the price of a castle at the time

In 1577 arctic explorer Martin Frobisher whilst on an expedition to the northern reaches of Canada made a remarkable discovery. He wrote the following in his journal -

"Upon another small island here was also found a great dead fish, which, as it would seem, had been embayed with ice, and was in proportion round like to a porpoise, being about twelve foot long, and in bigness answerable, having a horn of two yards long growing out of the snout or nostrils. This horn is wreathed and straight, like in fashion to a taper made of wax, and may truly thought to be the sea-unicorn."

When Frobisher returned to England, he presented the horn to Queen Elizabeth, who commanded that it be kept with the crown jewels.

Her successor James I was said to have paid a similar price for an alicorn. He chose to test the efficiency of its magical and restorative powers in a very severe way. He ordered that a servant drink a draft of poison with some of the unicorn horn added. Only when the poor servant dropped dead did the King declare that he had been deceived and that the horn was not genuine. I suppose that James earned his public moniker of "the wisest fool in Christendom".

As mentioned earlier, unicorn horns were exchanged as tributes. According to legend the horn on display at the Musée National du Moyen Âge was a gift from the Caliph of Baghdad, Harun al-Rashid, to Charlemagne in 807, quite an impressive piece that measures almost three meters in length.

Several unicorn skeletons have been discovered, but were proven to be fakes. In the 17th Century, a German Scientist and Inventor Otto Von Guericke wrote a newspaper article about the finding of some ancient animal bones in a large cave in Northern Germany. Gottfried Wilhelm Leibniz (1646-1716), a noted German polymath, drew a sketch based on the description which became included in a book of natural history written in the 18th Century.

Following the 1660 introduction of absolute monarchy in Denmark and Norway, King Frederick III (r. 1648–1670) ordered a Throne Chair to be created. It took nine years to make, by Bendix Grodtschilling a Danish painter and carpenter. The Throne Chair of Denmark is the physical representation of the Throne of the Kingdom of Denmark and of the Throne of the Kingdom of Norway. According to legend, the Throne Chair is made of the horn of unicorns. In reality, it is made from many pieces of Norwegian narwhal tusks. Today the Throne Chair is located in the Castle of Rosenborg in Copenhagen.

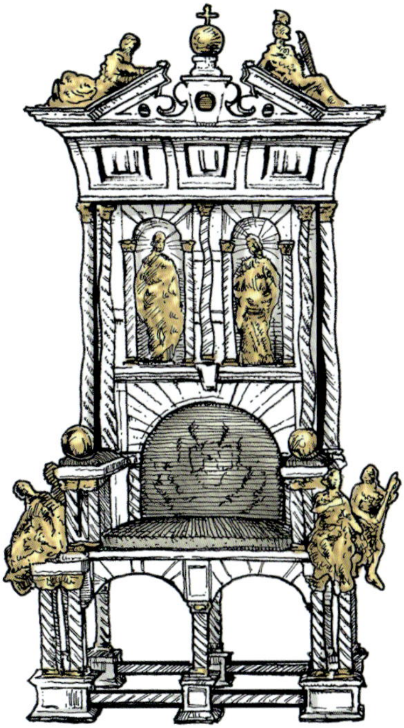

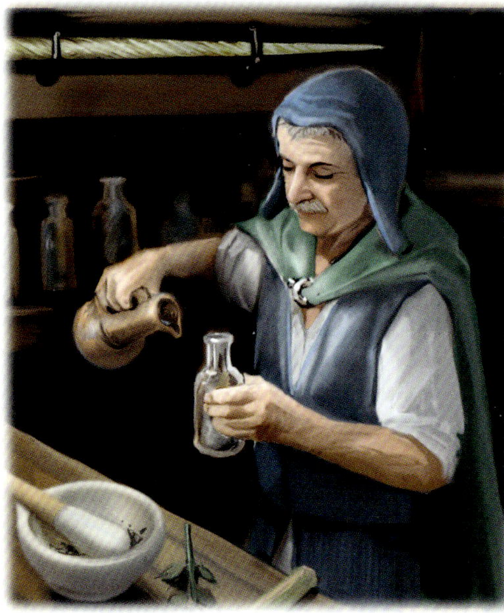

Apothecary is an old term for a medical professional who formulates and dispenses medicines to physicians and patients. The apothecaries' investigation of herbal and chemical ingredients was a precursor to the modern sciences of chemistry and pharmacology. As well as dispensing medicines, the apothecary offered general medical advice and a range of services that would nowadays be performed by specialist practitioners, such as doctors and even surgeons. In England, in the 17th Century, apothecaries' also controlled the trade of tobacco which at the time was imported as medicine. As such, the apothecaries themselves were revered members of society (as well as astute businessmen) and any advice given or remedy sold was certainly not up for discussion.

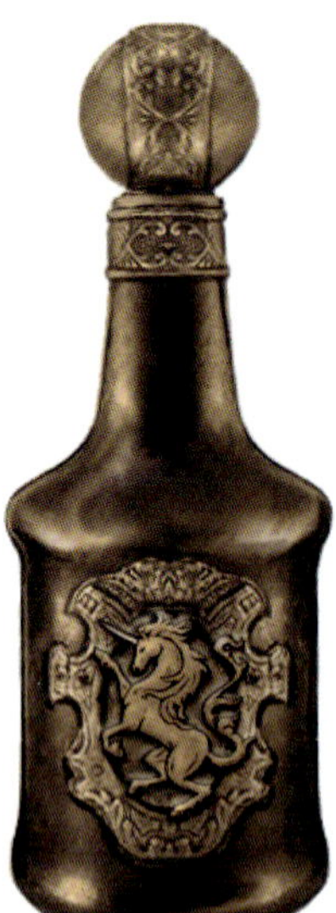

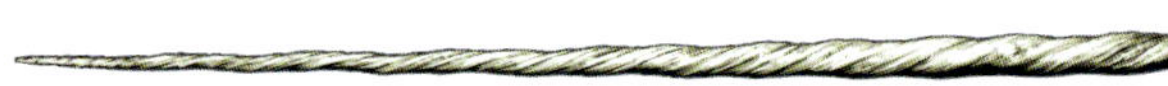

Due to the widespread belief in the healing horn, it was from the Middle Ages until the mid-18th Century that false alicorn powder (usually ground Narwhal horn) was sold throughout Europe for medicinal purposes. As such, the unicorn was the most recognizable symbol of an apothecary or pharmacy. Therefore, apothecaries had elaborate signs fashioned as unicorns; some of them even had real narwhal tusks. Others simply kept the tusks hanging above the door where patients could see them, thus assuring the public they had the 'real thing'.

APOTHECARY HERBALIST
ZEBEDIAH PRATTS
13 MORNINGTON TERRACE
HARROGATE

Now brought in use for the cure of all ailments by an experienced Doctor, the Author of this Antidote.

UNICORN HORN

A most excellent drink made with a true unicorns horn which shall effectively cure the following diseases:

Further, If any please to be Satisfied, they may come to the Doctor and view the Horn.

- Scurvy, Old Ulcers,
- Dropsy,
- Running Gout,
- Consumption, Distillations, Coughs
- Palpitations of the Heart,
- Fainting Fits, Convulsions,
- Kings Evil, Rickets in Children,
- Melancholy or Sadness
- The Green Sickness, Obstructions

And all distempers proceeding from a cold cause.

The use of it is so profitable, that it prevents diseases and infections by fortifying the noble parts, and powerfully expels what is an enemy to nature, preserving the vigour, youth and a good complexion to old age. No others can excel this, although they may claim to do, for it is only attainable with the infusion of a true unicorn horn to which it does corroborate and cure.

2. Also as a preparative for this excellent drink, and good against the diseases mentioned above and all crudities in the body, is ready prepared twelve pills in a box to be taken as three doses. According to directions therewith given, the price is 2/- the box.

INSTANTANEOUS CURE FOR ALL AFFLICTIONS

PRICED TO SELL - ONLY 2/- A BOTTLE

"A unicorn foal is gold at birth and without any vestige of a horn..."

CHAPTER III

Biology

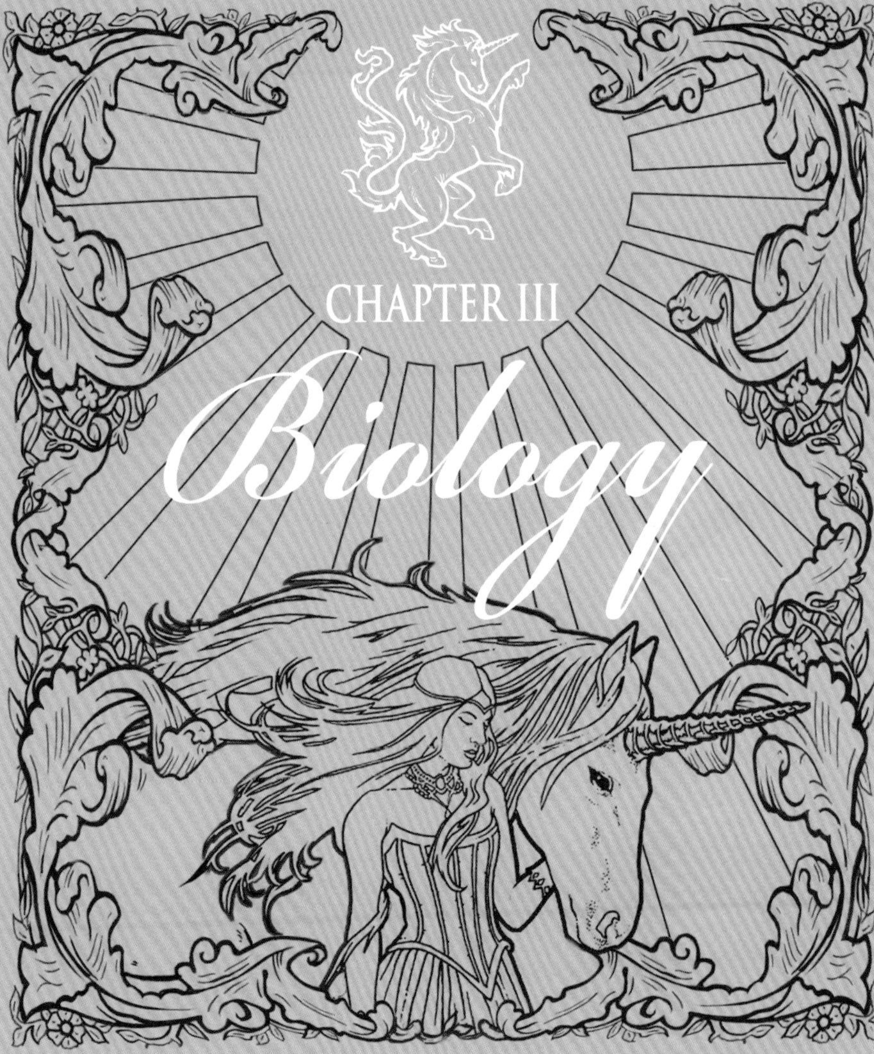

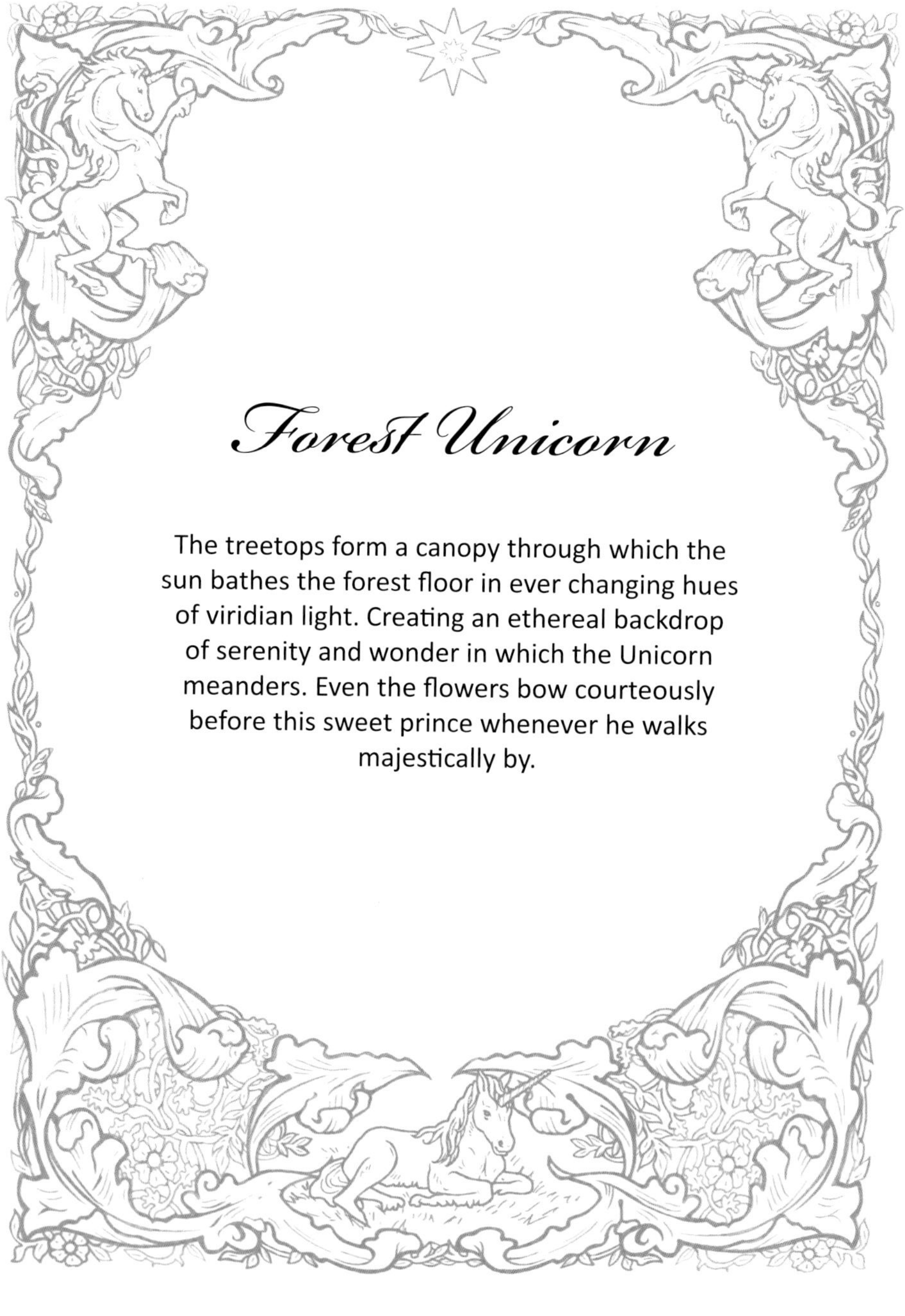

Forest Unicorn

The treetops form a canopy through which the sun bathes the forest floor in ever changing hues of viridian light. Creating an ethereal backdrop of serenity and wonder in which the Unicorn meanders. Even the flowers bow courteously before this sweet prince whenever he walks majestically by.

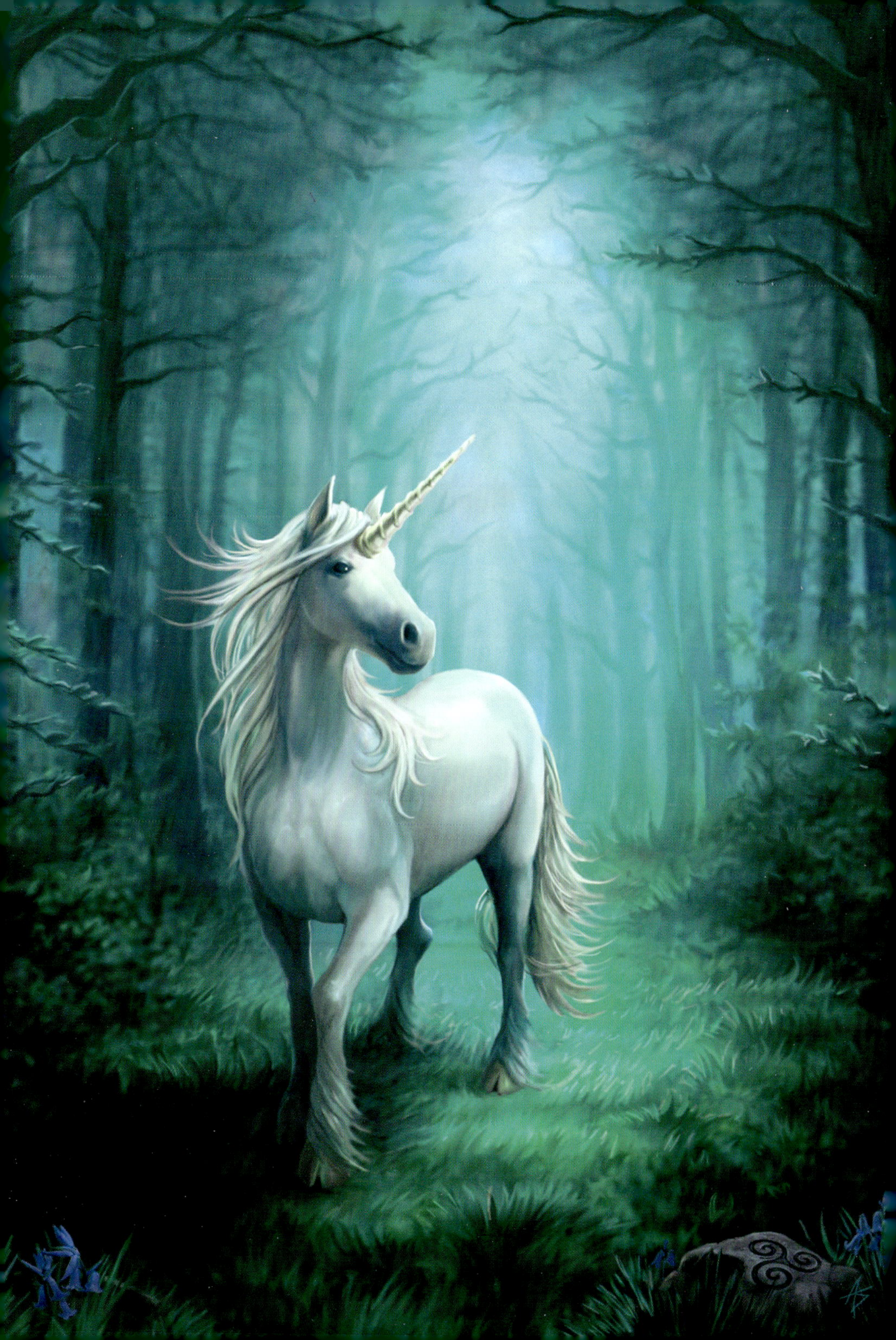

To date we have no supporting evidence regarding the zoology of the unicorn, although we can piece together salient features based on writings through the ages.

Reproduction

Sharing similarities to the members of the horse family, unicorns are highly social. Their social structure is unlike any other as there seems to be no mating rituals between full grown males, or a tendency to have an alpha male. We categorize the unicorns in the same terms as horses; male unicorns are born as colts and at three years old regarded as stallions. Females are born as a filly, they also on their third year become mares.

Unicorns are monogamous. Female unicorns mature earlier than the males, and a mare may have her first foal by the age of three. Stallions are not able to breed until the age of five or six. Mares give birth to rarely more than only one. She nurses the foal for up to a year. Also like horses, unicorns are able to stand, walk and suckle shortly after they are born. A unicorn foal is gold coloured at birth and without any vestige of a horn. This begins to develop around six weeks; three weeks later the colour changes from gold to pure white.

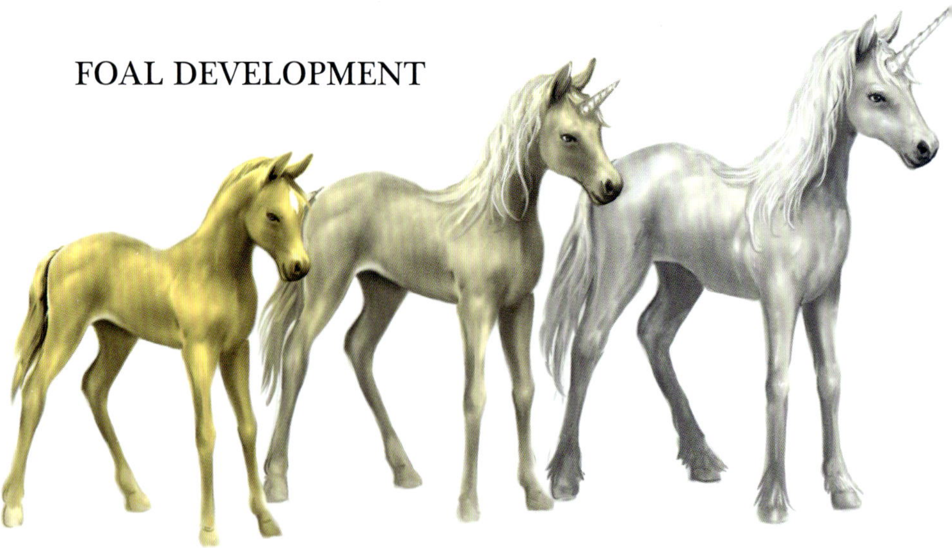

FOAL DEVELOPMENT

NEW BORN SIX WEEKS OLD NINE WEEKS OLD

Skeleton

The unicorn has a large skeletal system whose purpose is to protect the vital organs, maintains its shape, allows movement and gives points of attachment for muscles, tendons etc.

Regarding the bones; have you heard the expression "horses for courses"? Well, in regards to horses it means that a particular type of horse would be bred for a certain sort of job. One breed may do well in certain equine pursuits because of its body structure. Another, simply because of its size and bulk would not. We aren't surprised to see a Clydesdale pulling a plough over rough and uncultivated land. Or to watch a thoroughbred gliding effortlessly past the winning line at Royal Ascot. All breeds of horses are bred for a different purpose. So, what about a unicorn? Is it capable of, say, doing both those examples? Yes, indeed and so much more. That is because its bone structure is far greater than that of a horse. The major bones in horses are mostly tubular in shape. Whereas the unicorns' (although similar in length and diameter) thickness is greater, yet lighter, akin to titanium alloy which makes them around 5 times stronger than any horse. In short this means that they are able to run faster, leap, climb and drag heavy items more than any of an equine equivalent.

A slight difference in bone count; there are three extra Coccygeal or Caudal Vertebrae in a unicorn's skeleton structure compared to a horse. This enables it to have a longer and stronger tail.

Senses

Unicorns have excellent eyesight and it is believed that they can see in colour. Like most ungulates (hoofed animals), the unicorn's eyes are on the sides of its head, giving it a wide field of view. They have excellent night vision, comparable to an owl, enabling their pupils to capture lots of light. For example, a unicorn could probably spot a mouse at a distance in a forest lit only by a single candle.
They have excellent hearing and have larger, rounder ears than horses; similarly unicorns can turn their ears in almost any direction. In addition to superb eyesight and hearing, unicorns also have heightened senses of smell and taste.

Diet

It is believed unicorns feed almost entirely on grasses, but may occasionally eat shrubs, herbs, twigs, leaves and bark. Their unique digestive systems allow them to subsist on diets consisting of lower nutritional quality than that necessary for other herbivores we know of.

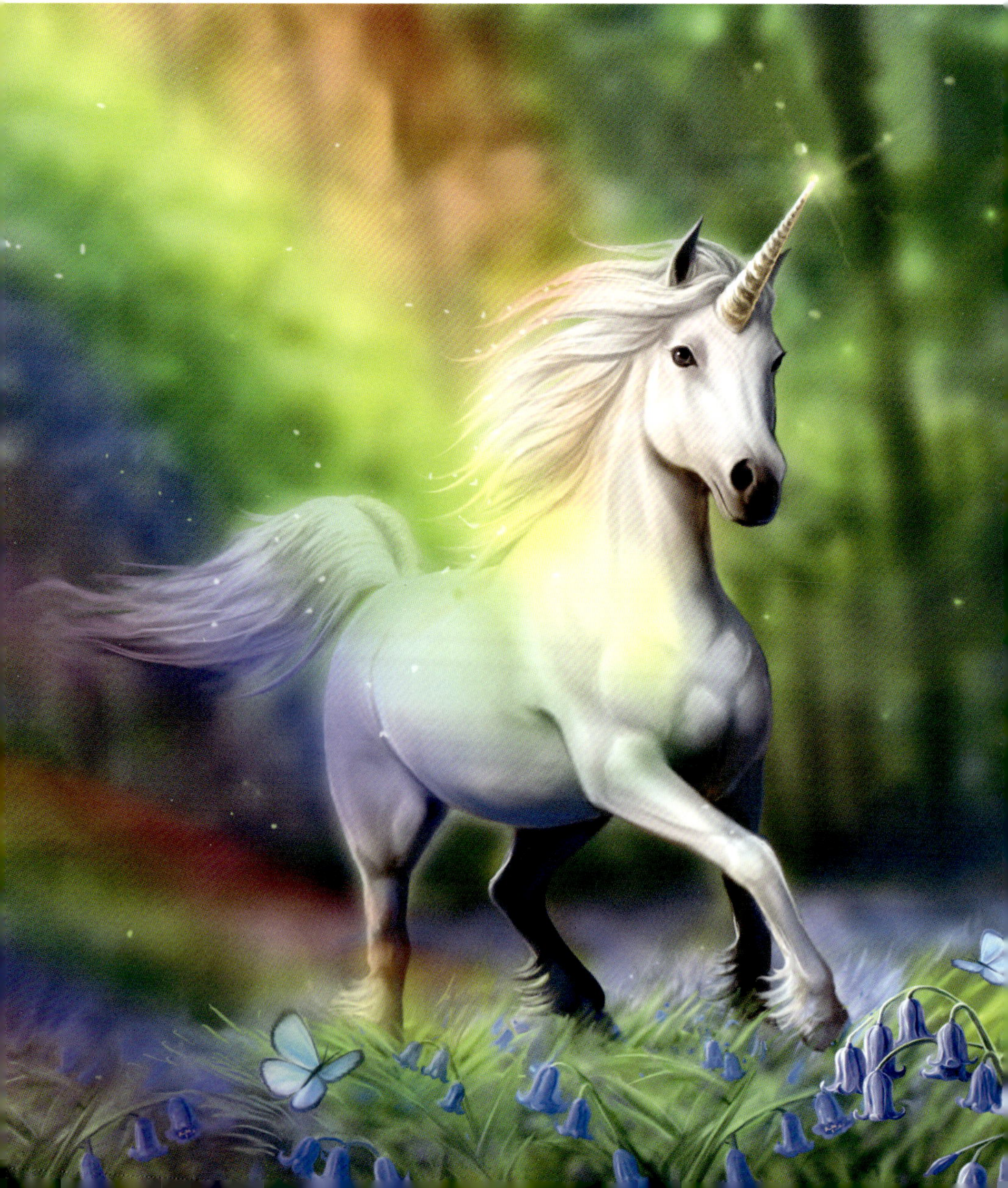

Hooves

Unicorns are able to able to handle a wide range of terrains, including steep inclines. They accomplish this solely through the way their special feet are developed under the outer carapace.

Their hooves are split into two toes, each of which can act independently. Each toe is shaped like a parabola on the outside, which adds strength, and it's soft in the middle, so the toes can deform and shape themselves to match the surface. The unicorn is able also to splay its toes to increase the contact area between its foot and whatever it's trying to scale.

Skin & Hair

By housing the hair follicles and melanocytes (melanin-producing cells located in the bottom layer of the skin's epidermis), the unicorn's skin also determines its colour. Unlike the three primary horse colour pigments: black, brown and yellow, the unicorn's is unique in being pure white.

It has three types of hair: permanent hair like his mane and tail, which grows and does not shed out; tactile hairs like whiskers; and the regular hair coat, which grows and sheds out with the stimulation of sunlight. As such its healthy skin and coat serves as an indicator for a unicorn's inner health, so you could say its beauty is more than just skin deep.

Due to the fine quality of its hair and the tight spacing within the skin it enables a high level of waterproofing. As such, the very tiny bubbles of moisture caught at the base of the hair follicles, when refracting light, gives a rainbow effect whilst the unicorn is in motion.

Life Span

Man is known to be the only predator of unicorns. As such has had a great impact on the unicorn population, if we are to believe the fanciful wishes of artisans of the Middle Ages. Unicorns were, and still are hunted for their horns (see section on Anatomy), skins and even their meat; although the latter is only able, by decree, to be eaten by royalty.

Thankfully there are no actual reported viable documents attaining to the actual killing of a unicorn. As such the unicorn is able to live out its magically enhanced life for hundreds of years.

"In European folklore it is said that a Unicorn may only be entrapped by the lure of a female virgin..."

CHAPTER IV

Capture

Blue Moon

Under the light of a rare blue moon, owls cry out and creatures of the night abound, a maiden rests alongside a Unicorn. In its protection she knows that she is safe from all things that would wish her harm. Only this bond of intimacy and trust provides comfort in this perilous midnight forest.

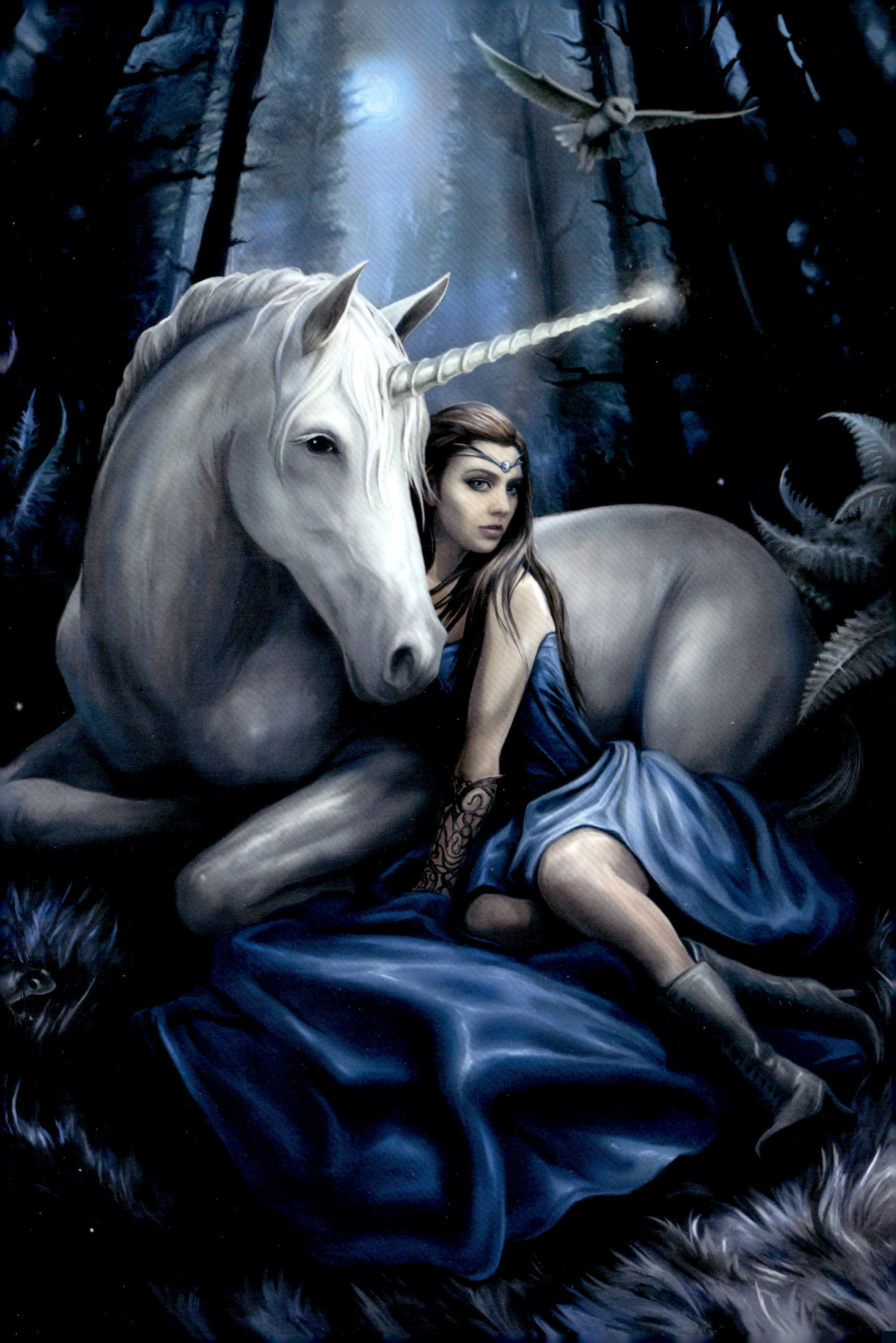

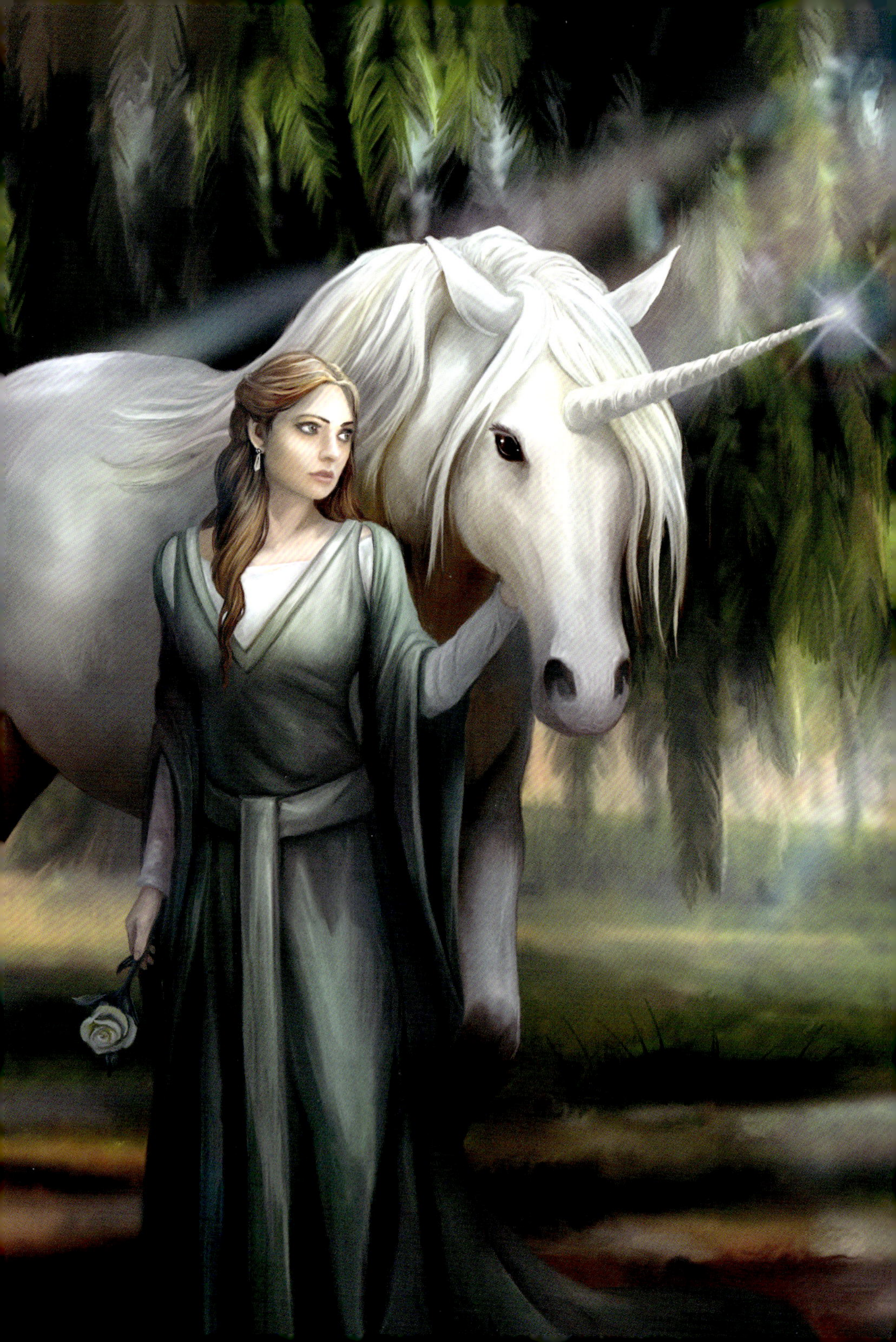

Man has always wanted to possess everything beautiful he sees; to capture and suppress something, it would seem, makes him feel superior. And something as magical and wondrous as the Unicorn becomes extreme in his desires. So, how galling it must have been that it was woman that could tame the beast, as it were. In European folklore it is said that a Unicorn may only be entrapped by the lure of a female virgin.

The precise definition of what an acceptable virgin is was subject to much interpretation however. Sources varied to say the least; she must be a nun, or, she must be of noble birth. It was a given that she must be physically attractive. She must be a total innocent without sin; she must be pure of heart; or that she must be a virgin in the purely sexual sense of the word.

Whatever the context it is documented that a maiden, either noble or poor, that is alone in a forest may attract the attention of a unicorn. Could it be that the beast has the ability to look into our hearts and minds? In doing so would it know if we meant harm to it or not? For as mentioned earlier, the unicorn is believed to be able to sense a liar.

It is for certain that for whatever reason the maiden needed to be on her own, she did not ask the unicorn to join her. For those women who formed an alliance with hunters wishing to kill the unicorn or cause harm to it themselves seldom returned from the forest. A passage written upon a 13th Century French manuscript currently in the Bibliothèque Nationale de France, Paris, states that a nobleman from the House of Normandy set out to capture a live unicorn. He enlisted the aid of a servant girl to lure the animal with promises of rich payment. She must have been besotted with him and readily agreed. After the planning she went alone and ahead of the band of hunters to sit in an area reported to be frequented by unicorns. When the nobleman and his men arrived at the scene they found no trace of the girl except for her headscarf. Despite a wide search of the province the girl was never seen or heard from again.

One can only hope that such an event dispelled the desire for hunting unicorns. A respite, as it was, against their endless pursuance.

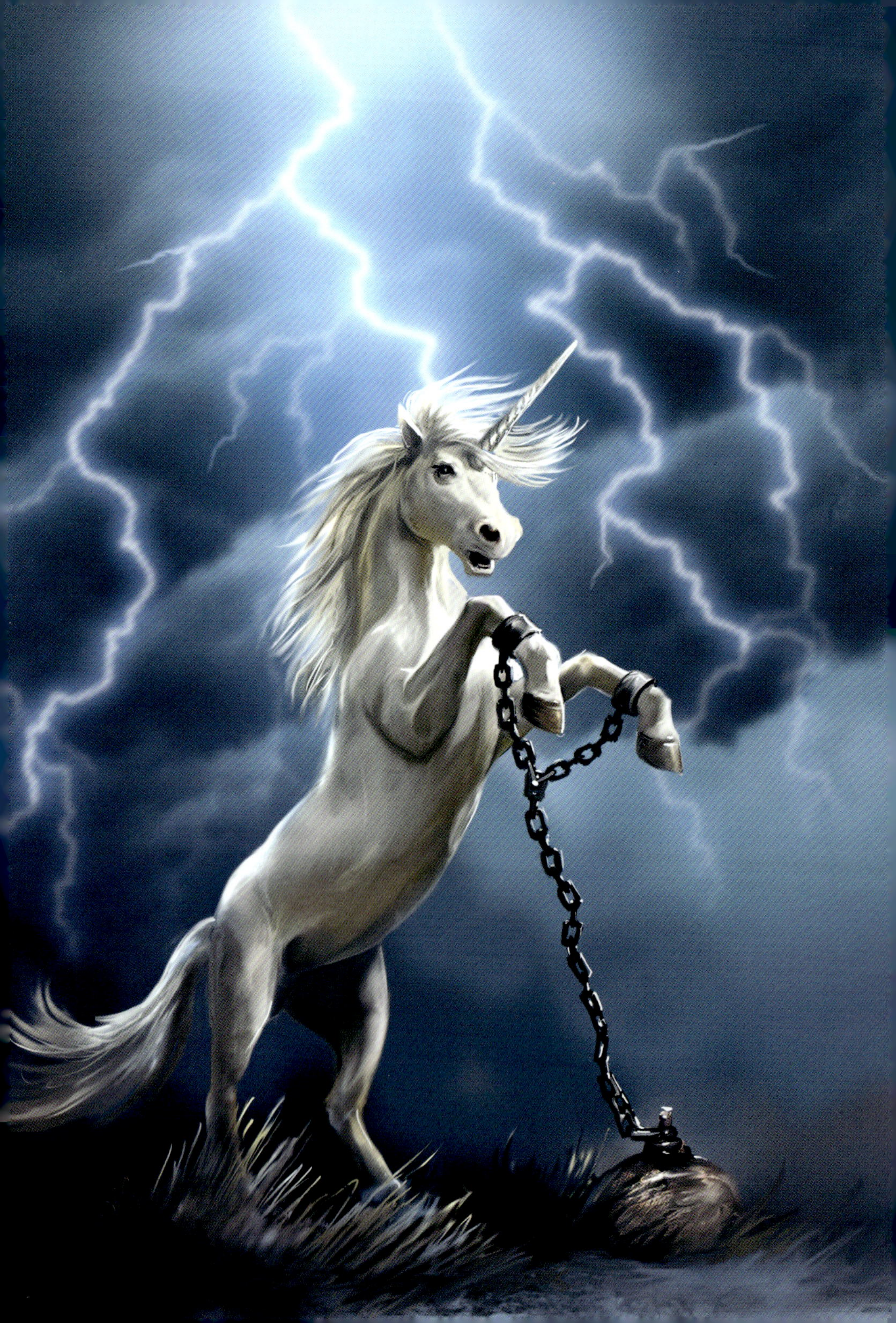

The documenters of medieval history had no problems with depicting, quite graphically, how the unicorn could be slain once enchanted by the maiden. Many bestiaries lovingly illustrated show them being speared, run through with swords, clubbed to death and even cleaved in-two. For a creature we acknowledge now as being kind and caring and certainly wouldn't cause harm, the medieval thirst for its extinction seemed to be insatiable.

Leonardo da Vinci (1452-1519) wrote -

"The Unicorn, through its intemperance and not knowing to control itself, for the love it bears to fair maidens forgets its ferocity and wildness; and laying aside all fear it will go up to a seated damsel and go to sleep in her lap, and thus the hunters shall take it."

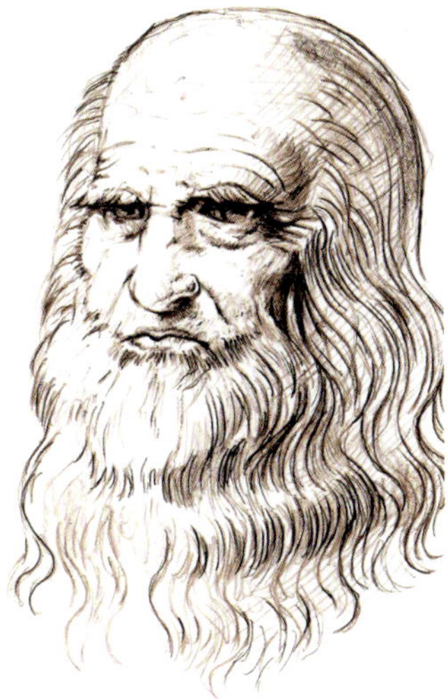

Another take on capturing it is suggested in **William Shakespeare's** 'Timon of Athens', Act 4, scene 3: *"wert thou the Unicorn, pride and wrath would confound thee and make thine own self the conquest of thy fury".* Which in essence is suggesting that if goaded, the Unicorn would make itself vulnerable through an ill-thought-out act born of rage?

Comparable to the actions in a medieval story found in a letter from a Christian King, in Ethiopia, around 1165. It claims that the unicorn and the lion are natural enemies, and that the lion kills the unicorn by a subtle ruse: it positions itself between the unicorn and a tree, and when the unicorn charges, it leaps aside. The unicorn's horn is thus plunged into the tree, and the unicorn cannot withdraw it. The unicorn is trapped, and the lion easily kills it.

The most well-known depiction regarding the hunting of a unicorn is not in fact a painting; it is a series of seven tapestries dating from between 1495 and 1505. Simply called 'The Hunt of the Unicorn', or the Unicorn Tapestries, they are considered by many to be the most beautiful tapestries in existence. Their origins and meaning are long lost and yet their splendour lives on. We do know that the unicorn was a symbol for many things in the Middle Ages, including Christianity, immortality, wisdom, lovers and marriage. They now hang in The Cloisters, part of the Metropolitan Museum of Art, New York, yet were probably woven in Brussels or Liège.

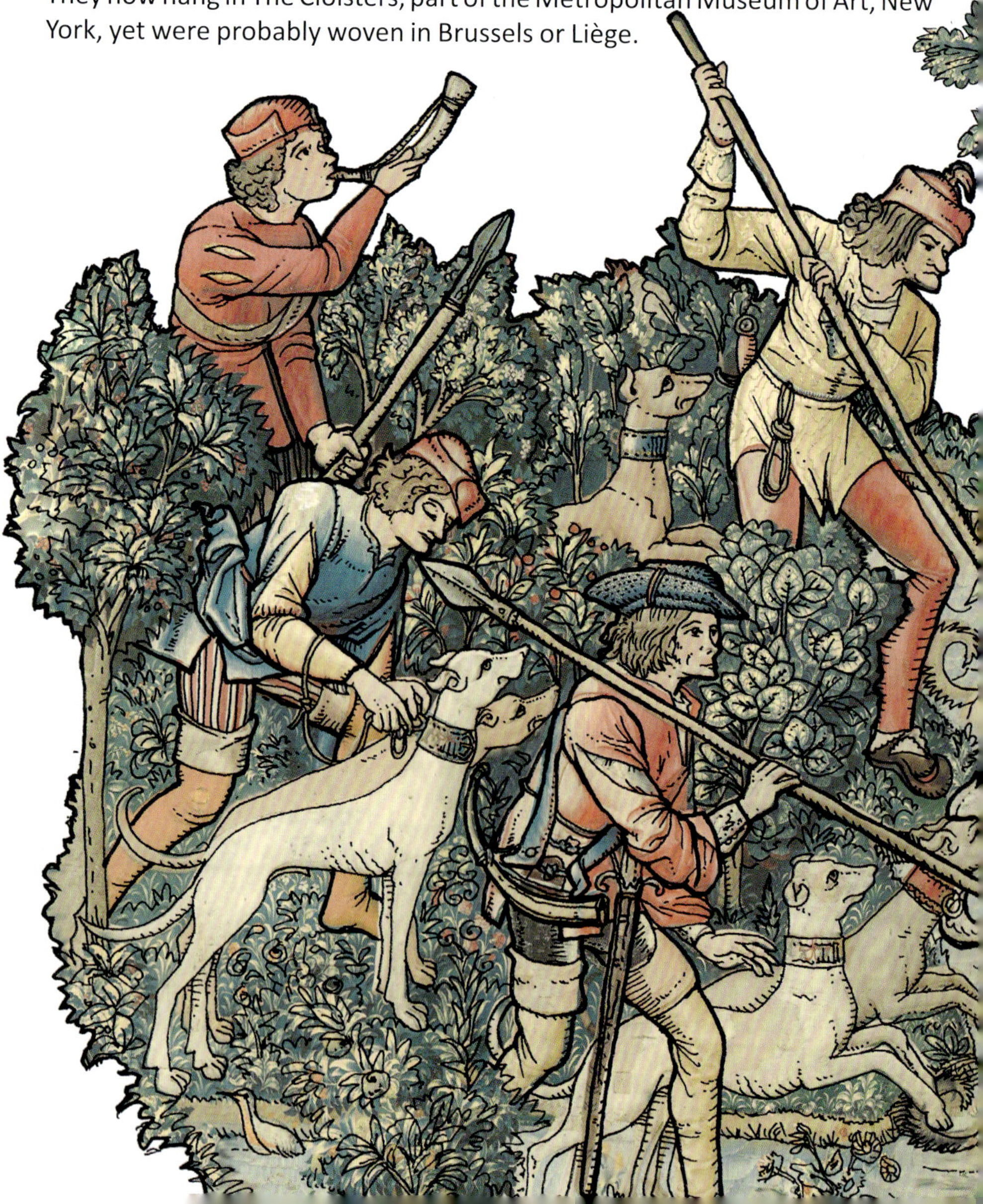

For centuries, the tapestries were in the possession of the La Rochefoucauld family of France. In 1922, John D. Rockefeller Jr., bought them for just over a million dollars and in 1937 he gifted them to the Cloisters. Their monetary value today is incalculable. They show a group of noblemen and hunters in pursuit of a unicorn. As mentioned earlier, the hunt for the unicorn was a common theme in late medieval and renaissance works of art and literature. The tapestries were woven in wool, metallic threads, and silk. The vibrant colours are still evident today and were produced from plant dyes. Unfortunately, only one of the panels 'The Mystic Capture of the Unicorn' survives as two fragments.

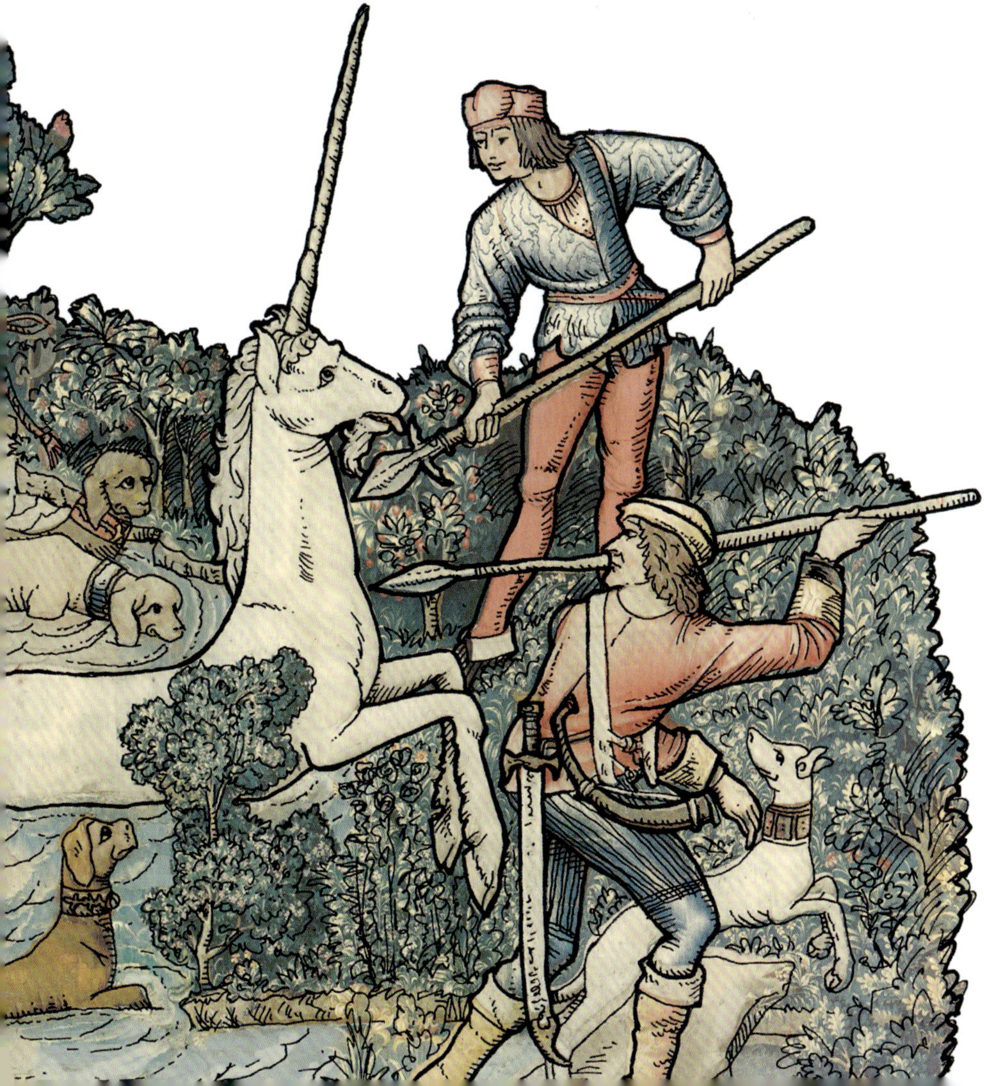

"The lion and the unicorn
were fighting for the crown..."

CHAPTER V

Heraldry

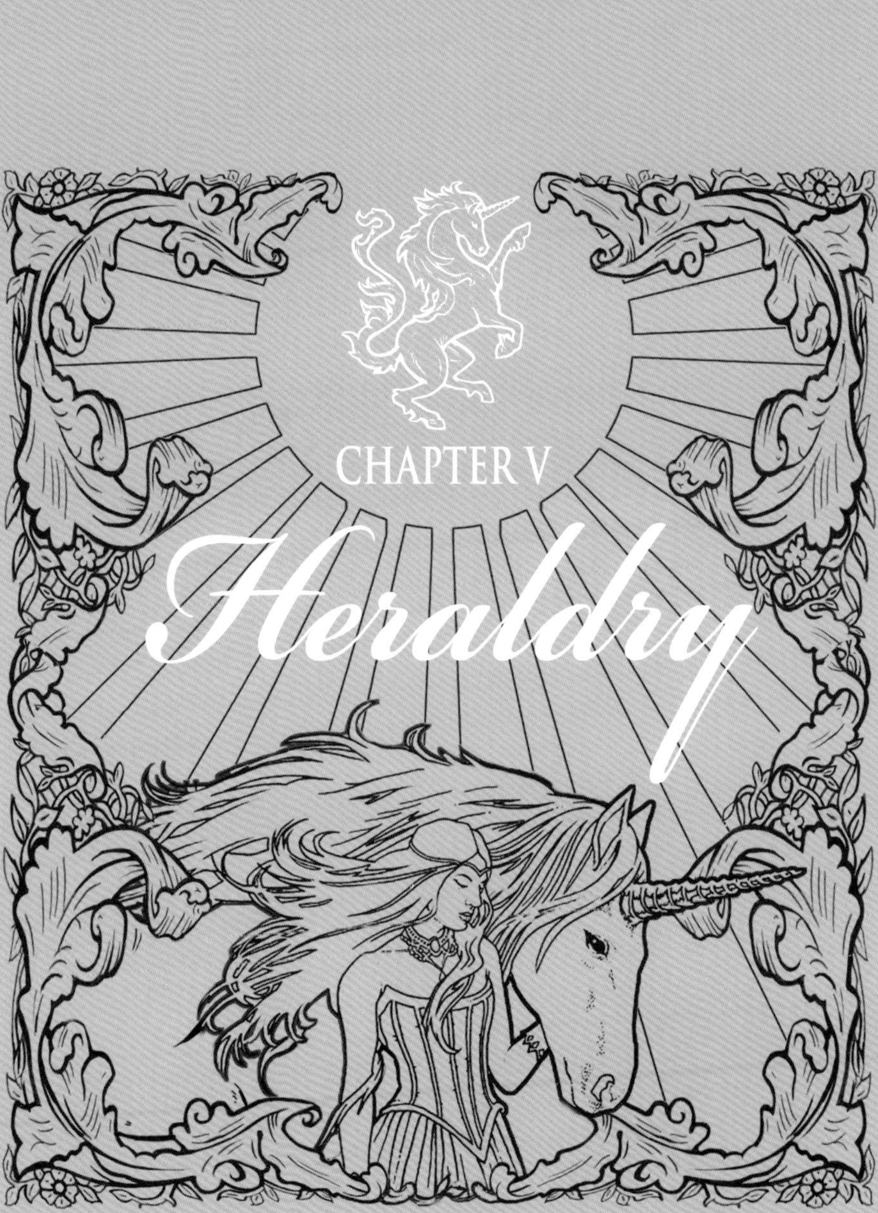

Enlightenment

Chains cannot hold it and neither can it be broken by the will of man. So in honour we use the Unicorns image to adorn many a sacred place. Although worship is not given in its name, strength is taken from all that the Unicorn stands for. Pure of heart and a symbol of courage, its image adorns the banner held aloft to fight the good fight.

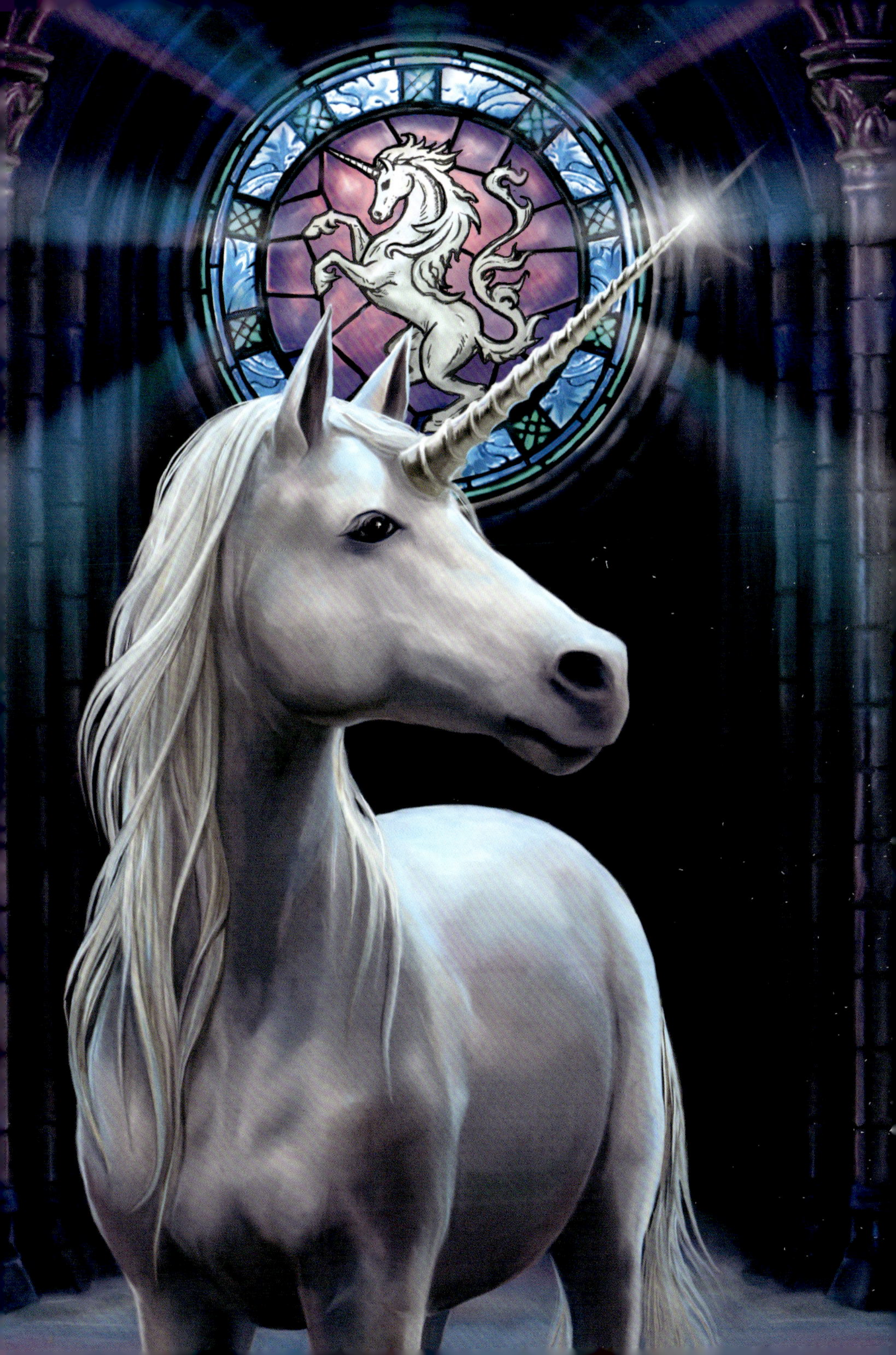

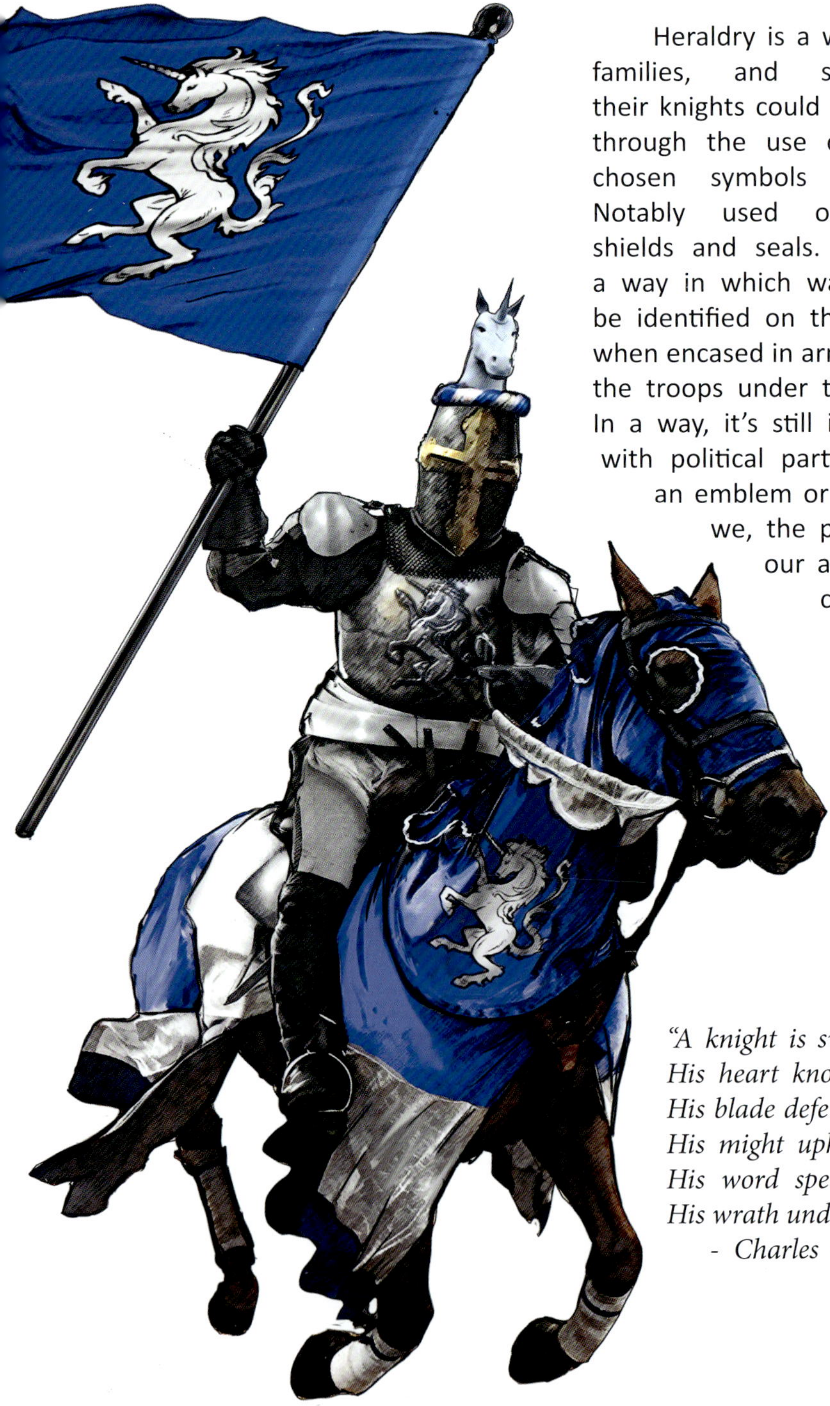

Heraldry is a way in which families, and subsequently, their knights could be identified through the use of particular chosen symbols and signs. Notably used on banners, shields and seals. It was also a way in which warriors could be identified on the battlefield when encased in armour, uniting the troops under the one flag. In a way, it's still in use today with political parties adopting an emblem or motif which we, the people, show our allegiance to come voting day.

"A knight is sworn to valour
His heart knows only virtue
His blade defends the helpless
His might upholds the weak
His word speaks only truth
His wrath undoes the wicked."
- Charles Edward Pogue

The heraldic unicorn may be traced back to when it began to figure prominently in church ornamentation. Worshippers were assailed subliminally by creatures of myth in the stone and wooden carvings around them at prayer. As such, a creature of God seemed only fitting to represent ones house. It consequently entered into the role in which it was to be most influential: heraldry.

Its popularity increased and the unicorn emblem is notably seen in insertion into coats-of-arms from the 15thCentury onwards. A side note here, as mentioned earlier, artistically at this point it became depicted with goat hoofs and a more slender tail. Surely it became representative as a symbol for purity, honour and virtue from then on.

John Guillim (1565- 1621), officer of arms at the College of Arms, London, wrote in his 'A Display of Heraldry':

"Some have made doubt whether there be any such beast as this or no, but the great esteem of his horn (in many places to be seen) may take away that needless scruple. The greatness of his mind is such that he rather chooseth to die than be taken alive: wherin the unicorn and the valiant-minded soldier are alike, which both condemn death, and rather than they will be compelled to undergo any base servitude or bondage they will lose their lives."

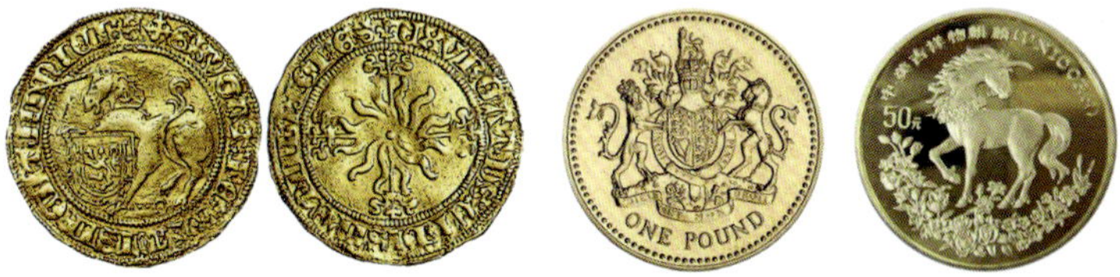

In Scotland between 1484 and 1525 there were golden coins called Unicorns and Half-Unicorns. It became the coin favored by Scottish kings when making gifts to foreigners. 500 years after the Scottish Unicorn coins the modern day British coinage also features the unicorn as part of their design in the nation's coat of arms, on what is commonly described as the 'tails' side of the coins. One of the more popular and heavily collected modern Chinese coins is the Unicorn; these mythical creatures were depicted on coins minted from 1994 - 1997.

Around 1426 King James I of Scotland (1394-1437) adopted the unicorn as the emblem for his country, as it represented a high and mighty beast that would rather die than be captured, just as the proud Scots would fight to remain sovereign and unconquered. To this day, the unicorn is the national animal of Scotland.

When James VI (1566-1625) became King James I of England and VI of Scotland on the death of Elizabeth of England in 1603, he ordered the drawing of new Royal Arms. This was to incorporate the lion of England as well as Scotland's unicorn.

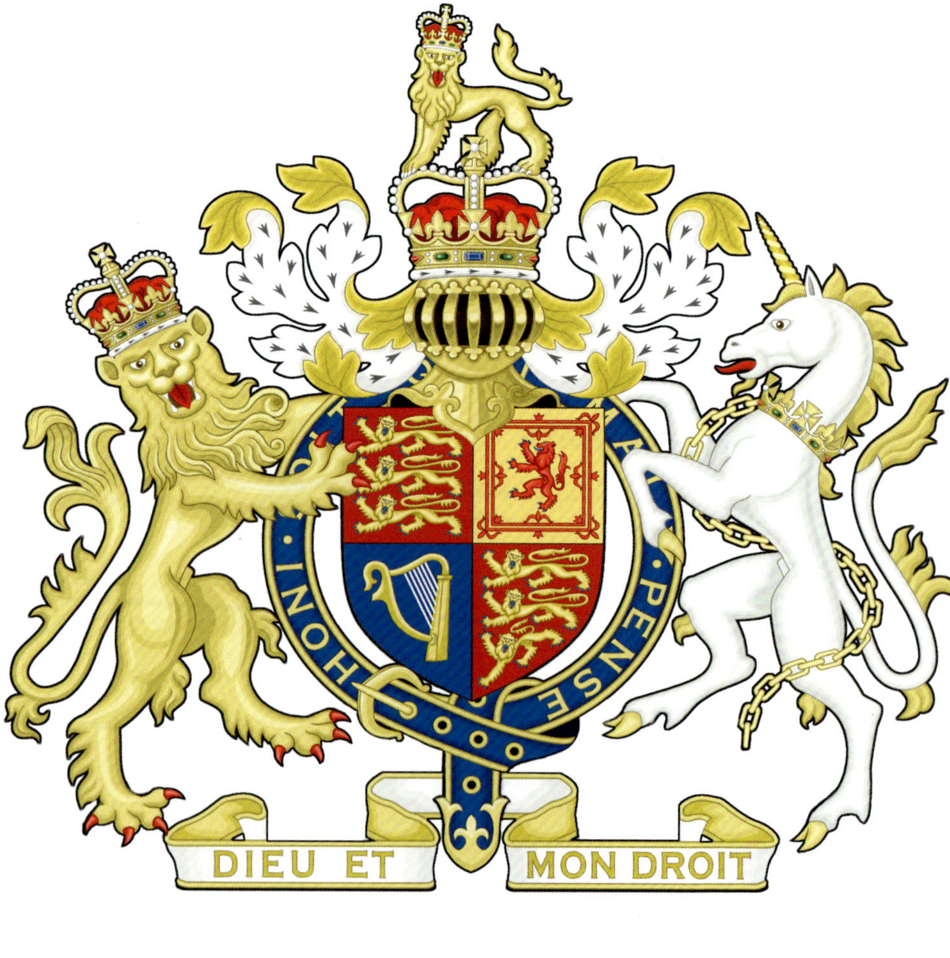

You may wonder why the lion wears the crown and yet the unicorn is chained? According to legend a free unicorn was considered a very dangerous beast; therefore the heraldic unicorn is chained, as were both supporting unicorns in the Royal coat of arms of Scotland.

It is an interesting note that the variation of the unicorn's long flowing tail is substituted for that of a lion's only in heraldry. A theory is that when it was adopted as the Royal coat of Arms the designer thought it more aesthetically pleasing to the eye if it balanced with the opposite lion.

The combination of the lion with the unicorn was not without mythological irony, for in folklore, the lion and the unicorn are sworn enemies, a tradition dating back to the Babylonians of 3500 BC.

A popular old English nursery rhyme sums up the hostility:

'The lion and the unicorn were fighting for the crown,

The lion beat the unicorn all around the town.

Some gave them white bread, and some gave them brown,

Some gave them plum cake and drummed them out of town'.

HMS Unicorn, of 46 guns, was built for the Royal Navy in the Royal Dockyard at Chatham and launched in 1824. She is now the World's last intact warship from the days of sail, one of the six oldest ships in the world and Scotland's only representative of the sailing navy. The ship has a carved unicorn sculpture at the bowsprit.

Such is the history and symbolism in the unicorn, its distinctive spiraling horn can be found in heraldry throughout the world from Brazil to Russia, an example pictured here in the Arms of Schwäbisch Gmünd, Germany. Many military forces have also adopted it as their insignia. These included the 359th Fighter Group and British Airborne Units, who both won major victories during WWII.

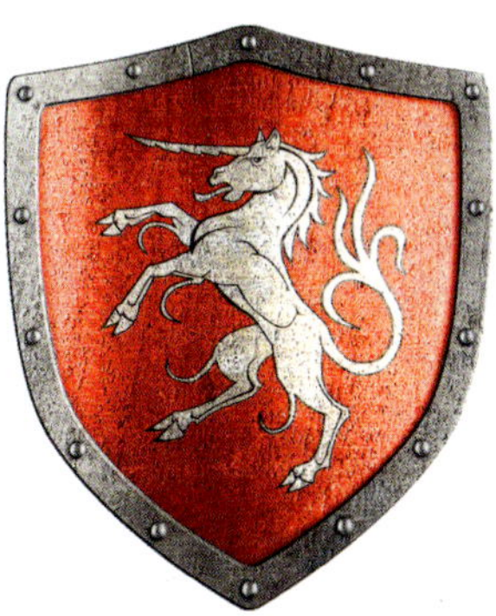

Journey's Start

A quest to right the wrongs has begun
The mage upon her mystic beast astride,
It is he that navigates the path ridden
His magical horn aids the perfect guide.

Neither knows how long it will take
Strength shall always be undiminished,
Whilst evil in the land remains awake
In unity shall they see it vanquished.

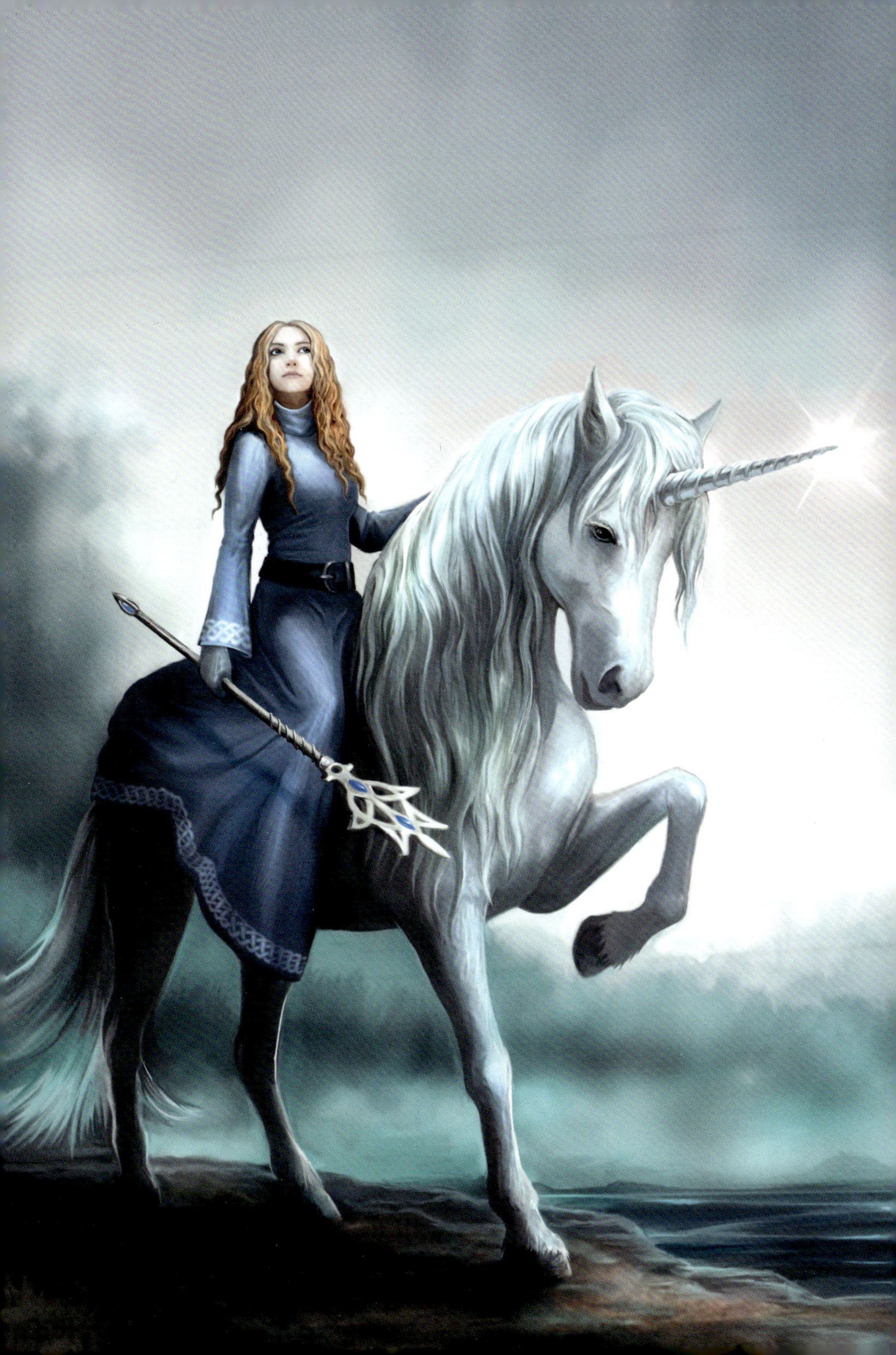

"Above all else the unicorn is a symbol of magic, miracles, purity, innocence and enchantment..."

CHAPTER VI

Spirituality

Glimpse of a Unicorn

The late summer days roll ever closer to autumnal breezes from the north. In a clearing in the forest, motes dance between sunbeams falling through ever widening gaps in the canopy. As if created by the light, a figure steps into view. But before the eye has time to assess this vision, is gone. Its path followed hither and thither as it wends its magical way into another realm.

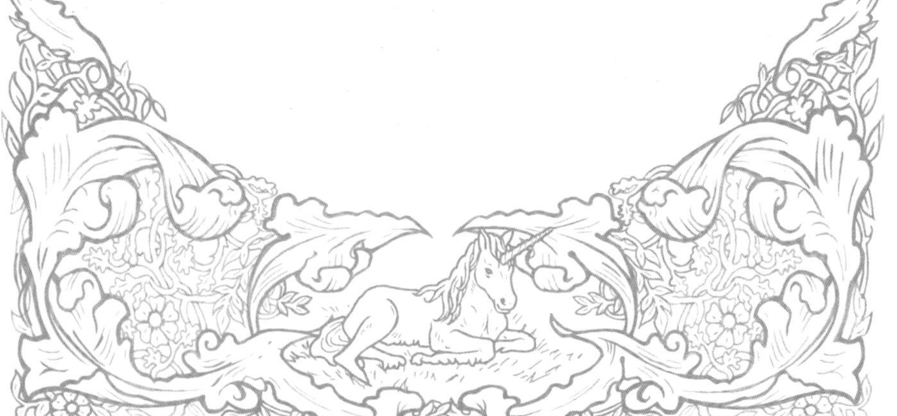

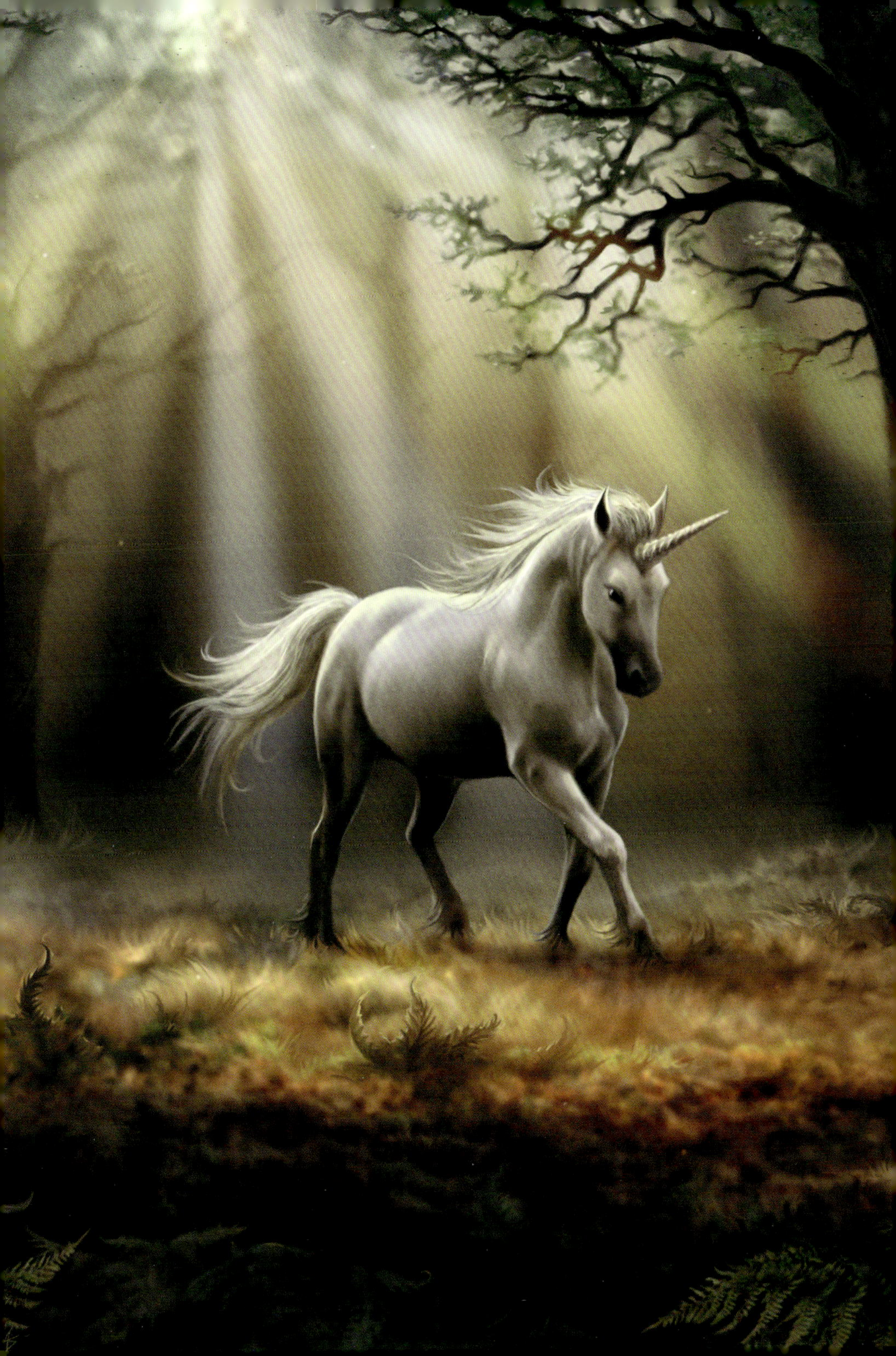

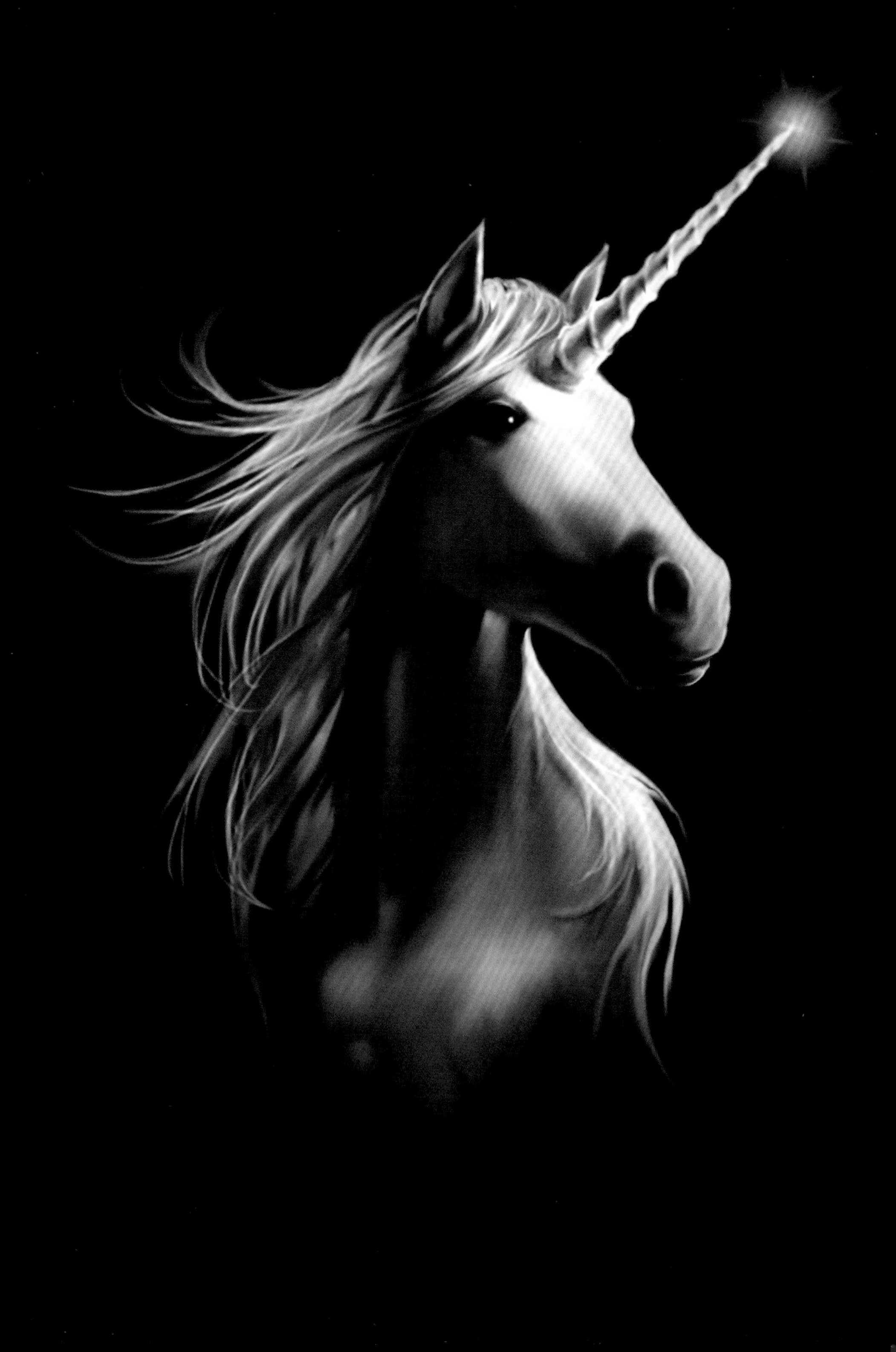

There are those that believe the Unicorn is a creature born between two worlds; our world and the next life. And that at the moment of its death it ceases to exist in ours, thereby leaving no proof of its existence except in legend. It is also believed to aid those that have passed and to be a spirit-guide into the afterlife. In China, the unicorn was called Chi lin, meaning yin and yang.

Above all else, the unicorn is a symbol of magic, miracles, purity, innocence and enchantment. Spiritually it appears to only a rare few and has the ability to bestow magic and wisdom to only those who are pure of heart and virtuous in their deeds.

It is believed that the appearance of a unicorn is accompanied by a soft and faint tinkling sound. As if a tiny bell were being shaken or of delicate chimes being caressed by a breeze. For centuries bells and chimes have symbolized the presence of divinity. For that reason the tinkling sound which accompanies the nearness of a unicorn reminds us that we are in the presence of a spiritual being, whose boundless domain are infinite and that we are truly blessed.

The unicorn seen within a forest represents purity and enchantment amidst growth, birth, rebirth, renewal and fertility; which are all feminine essences. Consequently, to slay a unicorn would be to wipe out a divine incarnation of innocence and perfection.

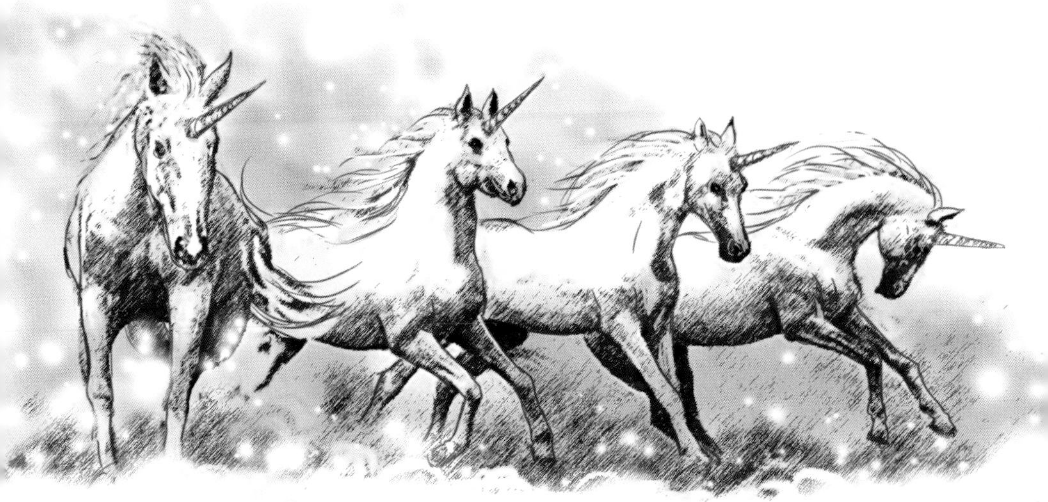

There are three symbols contained in the unicorn: the colour, the horse and the horn:

White is the colour of innocence, purity and perfection; which represents the lunar, instinct, intuition and virginity. Virginity in its truest metaphysical and alchemical aspect represents the untainted mind and spirit; it is the 'prima materia' (the pure matter) and the 'prisca sapientia' (ancient wisdom). It is for this reason that to have a unicorn appear before us is a divine gift.

The horse has always been regarded as a symbol of travel and movement. As the unicorn is a 'spiritual horse' it has the ability to travel and appear where and whenever it wishes. It is able to move throughout all realms, space and dimensions; between this life, the next and beyond infinitely.

The unicorn's single horn informs us that its domain is the realm of unity; a realm that transcends and exists beyond the bounds of matter and duality. Its single, spiralled horn is a symbol of the endless repeating cycles of time. It is also representative of the sword, and as the sword symbolizes the mind, the unicorn's horn also signifies unity of thought. Its horn protrudes from the top of its head, which is the location of the crown chakra.

The crown chakra is a border between realms. Representing the highest level to which our mind can attain and is the gateway to the higher realms of spirituality and divine consciousness.

The alchemical writings of Lombardi and others are often illustrated with pictures of the unicorn. They associated it with the 'third eye', the attainment of Nirvana and in philosophy to the Monad (the totality of all things).

Spiritually, the unicorn symbolizes success. If you were able to summon the power of the unicorn it would give you the blessings to be a success in whatever you chose to pursue. Possibly why 'unicorn' has now entered the world of high finance as a term used by Wall Street to denote start-up companies that have been valued at $1 billion or more.

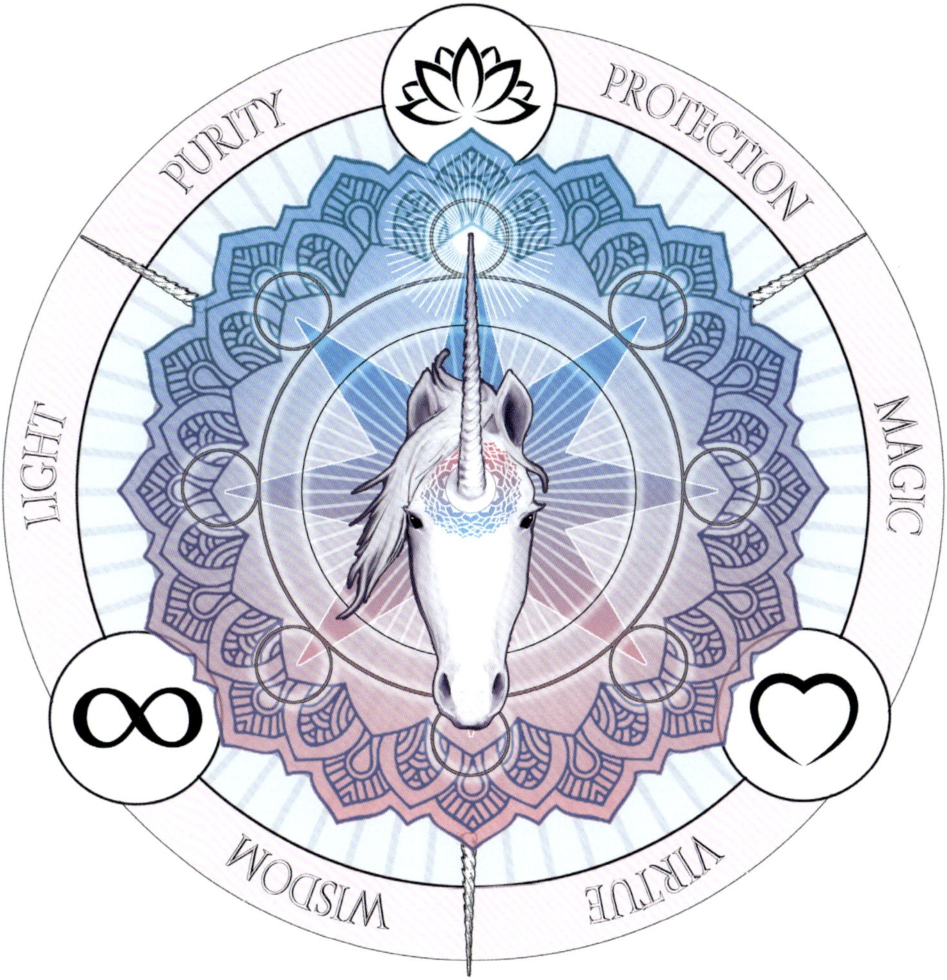

Spirituality is a broad concept and can be addressed from many perspectives. Generally, it includes a sense of connection to something bigger than us, understanding it typically involves a search for meaning in our life. It is very much a universal human experience, something that affects us all. To focus on the unicorn is said to be a spiritual experience and offers a peace and transcendence over the problems we may be facing.

So, as you see the symbolism of the unicorn is quite deep and yet pure and magical. Do you feel pure and virtuous enough to have a unicorn appear before you? That is a question we should ask ourselves each day as a metaphor for doing the right thing spiritually.

North Star

We stride at the very edge of the world
across these icy tundra's we've been guided,
I know that as long as you are here
there is no fear of the unknown.
For whatever lies ahead I know that
I can face it with you by my side,
And that thought comforts and warms me in
this place which seems forever in dark.

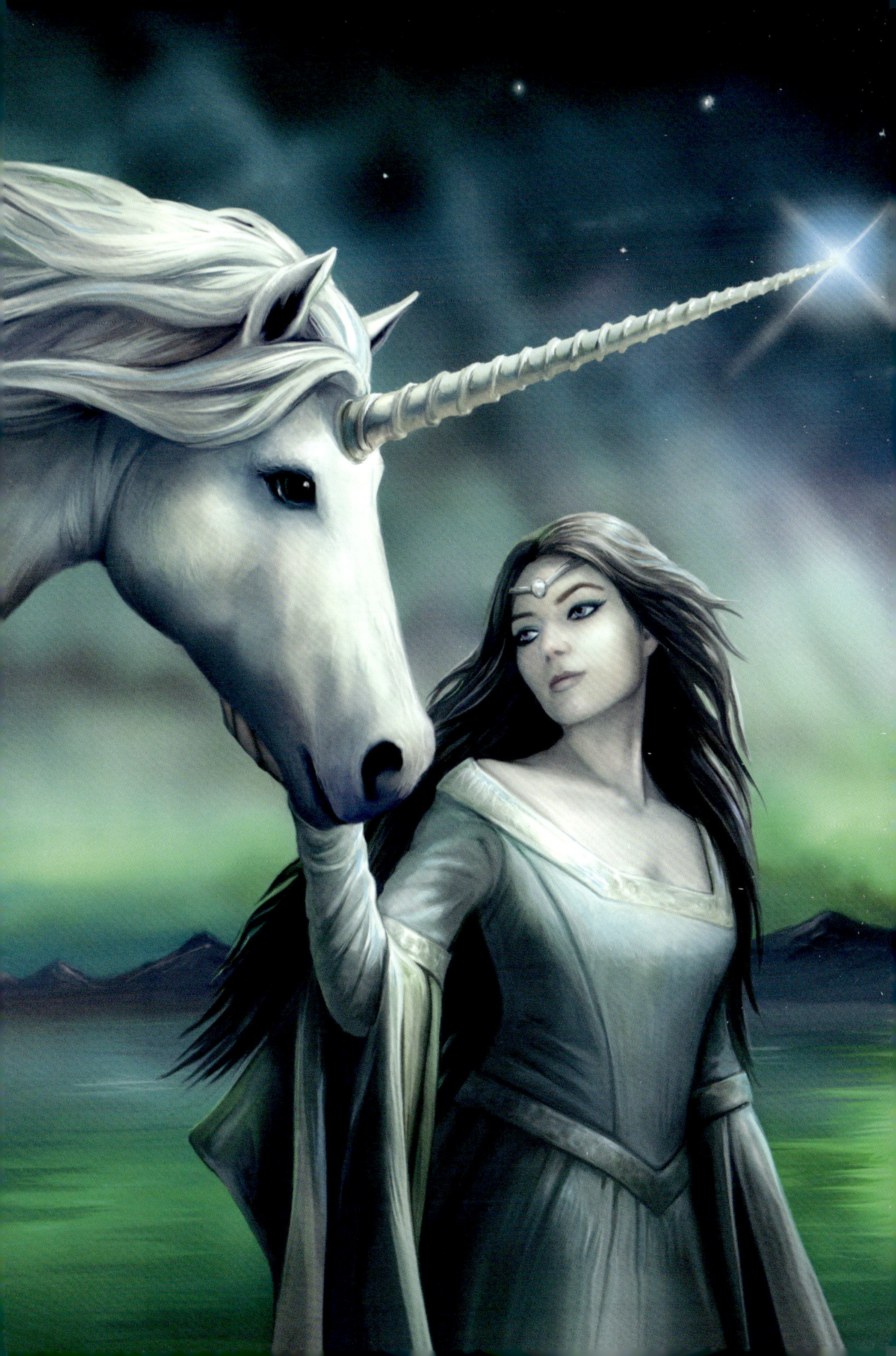

The High Mistletoe

Story by John Woodward

The basket was virtually empty and only a few wind fallen pieces of mistletoe had been found. The girl knew that if she returned with only this, then the man they called master would not be happy. To make matters worse, the snow began to fall heavier. Now, snowflakes as big as her small hands began to add layers very quickly to those that had fallen earlier that morning. And it was beginning to make walking through it hard.

A robin alighted on a branch nearby and proceeded to watch her. She stopped to blow on her frozen fingers, although it didn't seem to help. The robin caught her attention with a single sweet note and the girl stopped blowing and watched the bird as it flitted to a higher branch and then on to another. It then stopped, ruffled its feathers and with a song that seemed to say to her, "Here you are", then flew away.

Her eyes focused to just behind where the little robin had been. And there was the largest bunch of mistletoe the girl had ever seen. All thoughts of cold were forgotten and she laid her basket down. Having not taken her eyes off the prize, she held no fear, other than that of the master's wrath, as she began to climb. Her boots had been the property of many children before her and were indeed more cloth-wrap than leather. Undeterred, she placed her right foot against a gnarly knot and pushed herself up flat against the bark. The lowest branch was now within reach and with all the strength she could muster, pulled herself up. Stoically she climbed ever higher until at last reached the bunch of evergreen leaves with their pearlescent white berries.

At this height, the icy wind seemed to cut right through her and it was only now having reached her prize that she became aware, glancing down, how high she was. Her heart skipped a beat. She realised that the wind wasn't going to stop or the snow cease falling. She leaned forward, took out the small worn pruning knife she'd be given and began to cut at the base of the mistletoe. The snap of the branch rang out like a shot in the blizzard.

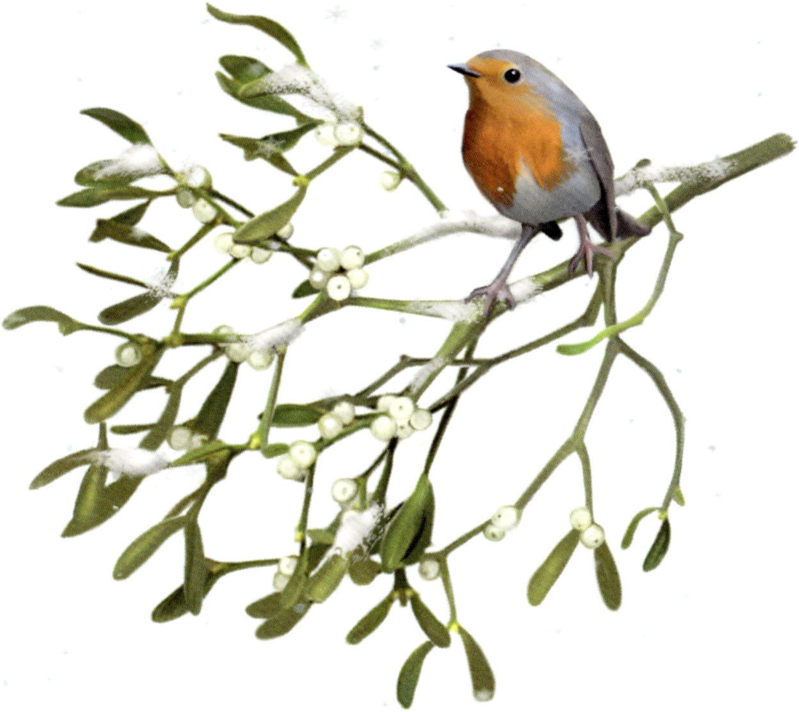

As she began to fall, the wind seemed to disappear and the snowflakes stopped in mid-air. She could see their beautiful lace-like patterns with such clarity, so lovely she thought. And then the ground knocked the very breath from her body and her little body lay so still with eyes wide open and fixed upon the heavens.

How long she laid there she didn't know. The sky above was still grey, but now no wind blew nor did snow fall. The icy cold no longer hugged at her as it had and an all over warm feeling comforted her. She continued to lie there. Then she heard the noise, so gentle, of something approaching leisurely. She really didn't want to sit up to look around; she was far too comfortable and so warm. And so she just rolled her eyes to the top and slightly tilted her head back. She smiled to herself when it came into view, albeit upside-down, and approached her. It too seemed to her that it smiled a little smile as it looked down at her. It was so bright that it seemed to glow against the grey canopy of the sky.

"Hallo", she said out loud and unabashed.

And in her mind she seemed to hear it say it back to her.

It seemed very impolite to just lie there and yet she did. It was so hard for her to want to break that feeling of comfort. Finally and with their eyes never leaving one another's, she rose unencumbered from the ground. Even standing the majestic beast to her was very tall and the single horn that extended from its forehead gave it extra height. She raised her arm, unafraid, the Unicorn lowered its neck. The girl gently stroked the soft mane.

With ease it lowered itself down, first onto one knee and then both. She knew it was an invitation for her to climb upon its back and she did.

"Are we going far?" she asked, as it rose. Again in her mind the answer seemed to say "Not far, little one, just a little way".

The following day the skies were a clear azure blue and the snow created a picturesque wintery landscape. The small group that had been assembled to look for the missing girl now stood around the small, oddly shaped mound of snow at the base of the old tree in silence. As the group left, following the master who carried the little girl's lifeless body, no one saw the robin land on the lowest branch. Nor heard its sweet high warbled lament, or witnessed its tear that fell upon the trampled snow.

The End

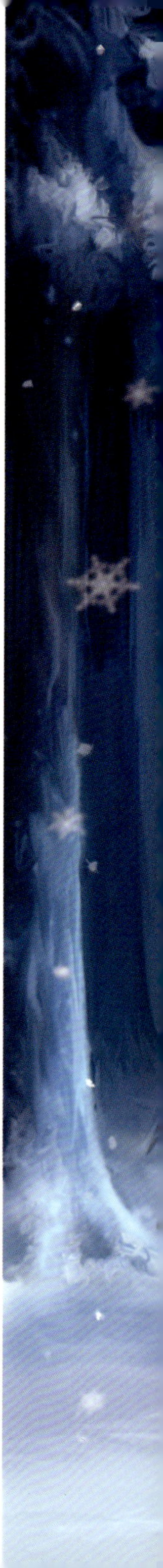

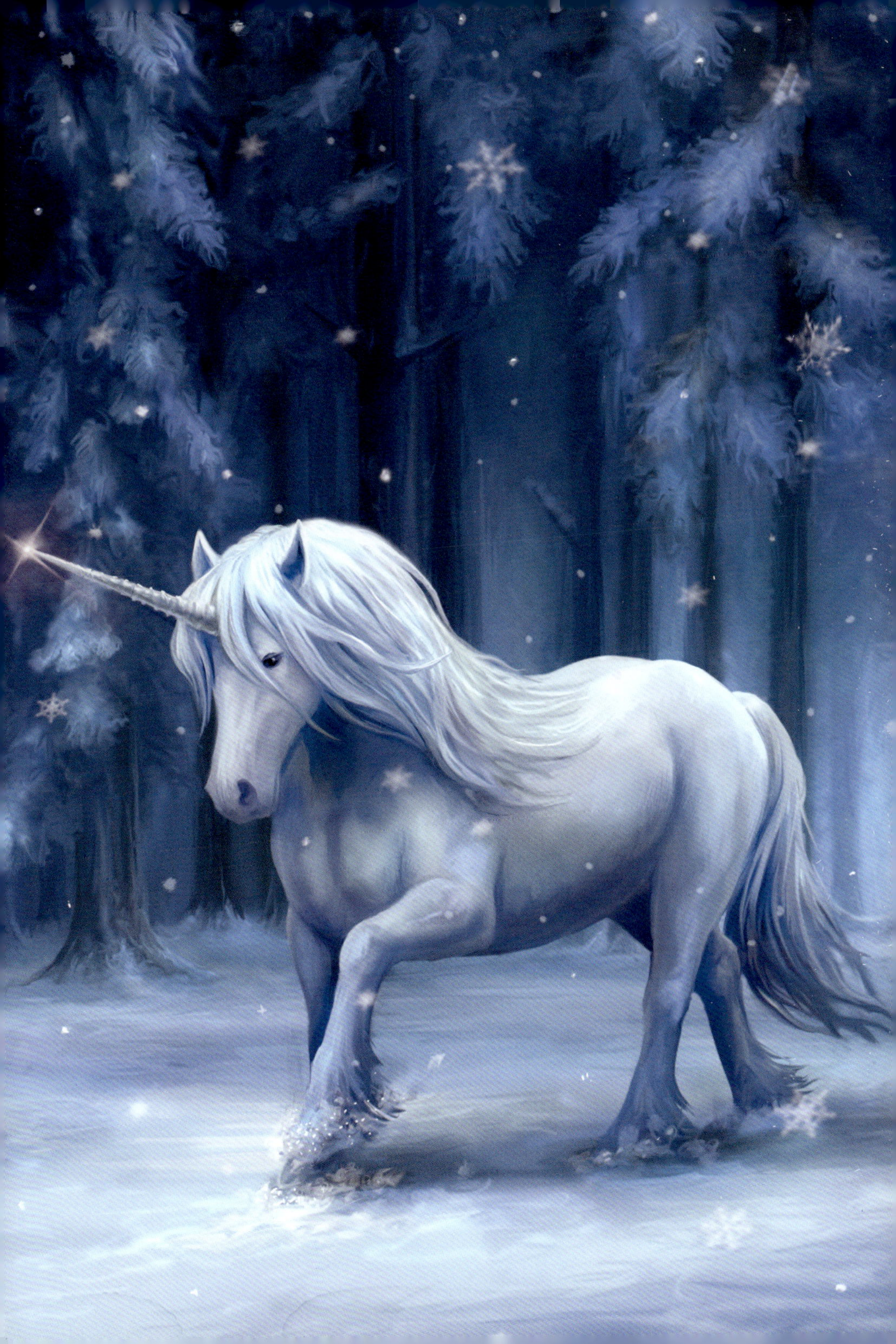

"Magick is neutral, neither good nor evil..."

CHAPTER VII

Magick

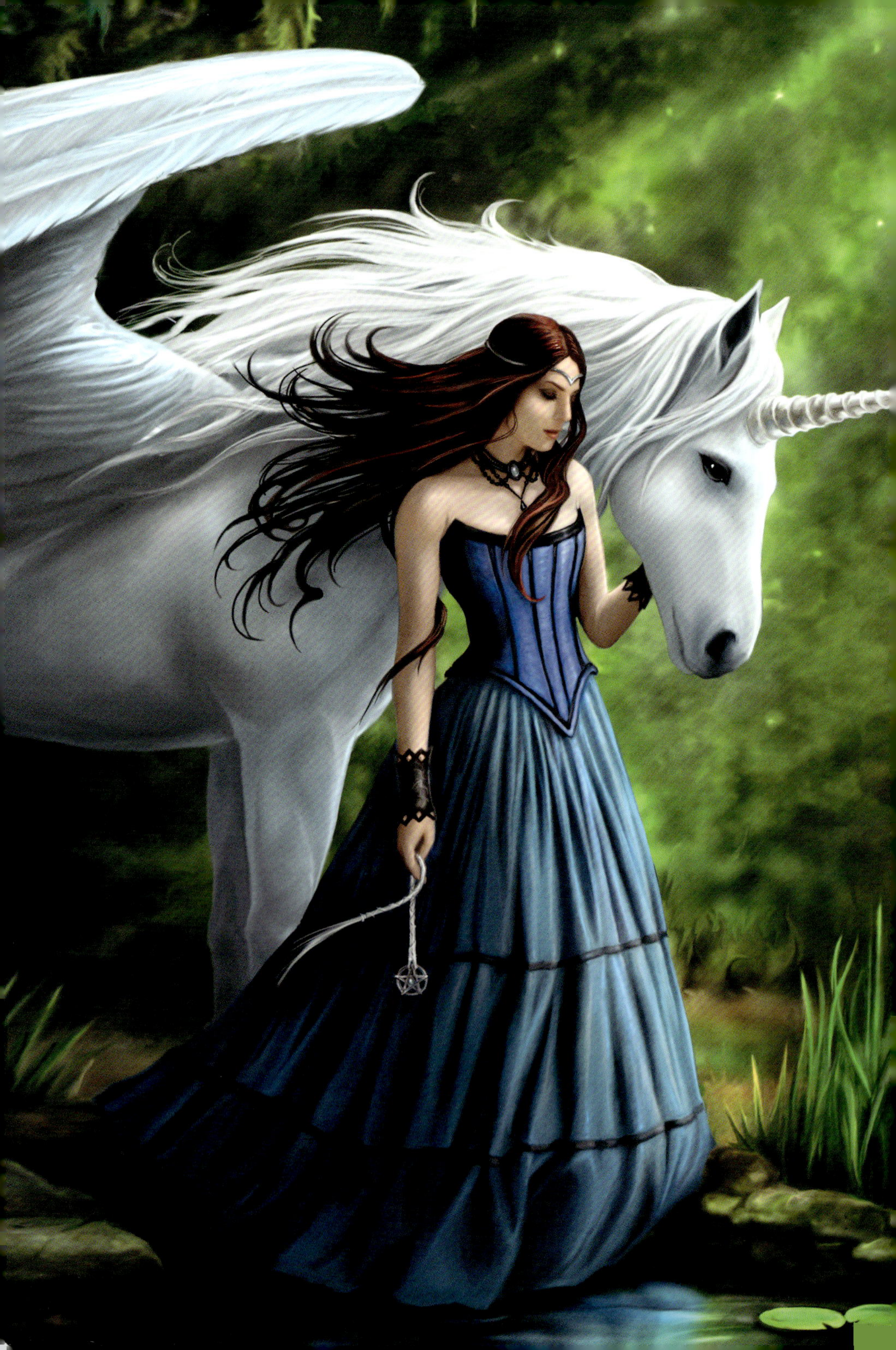

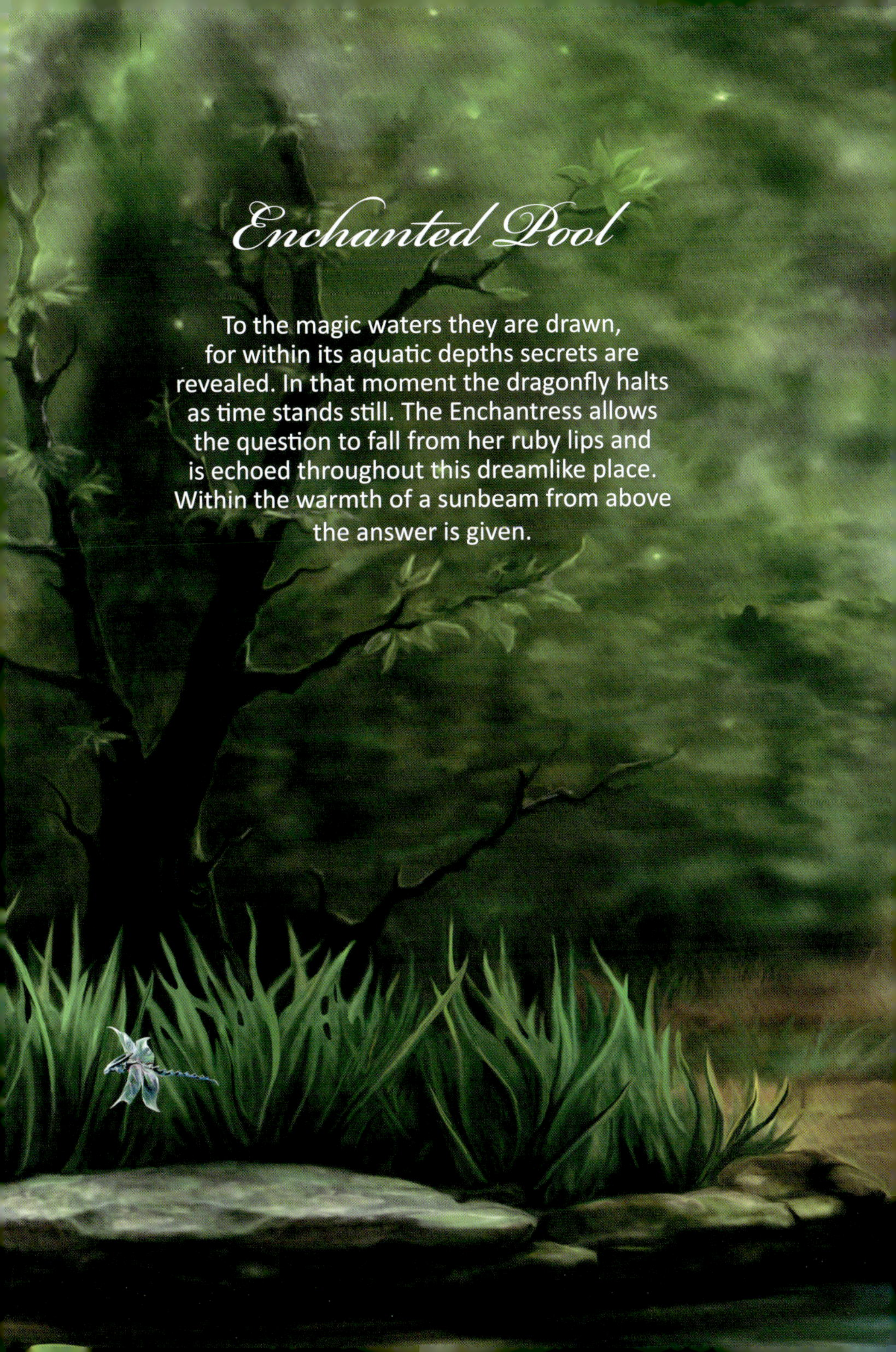

Enchanted Pool

To the magic waters they are drawn, for within its aquatic depths secrets are revealed. In that moment the dragonfly halts as time stands still. The Enchantress allows the question to fall from her ruby lips and is echoed throughout this dreamlike place. Within the warmth of a sunbeam from above the answer is given.

The unicorn has always been associated with magick, and that isn't a spelling mistake. Adding the 'k' to magic is not merely a quirk. Rather, it is a way to discriminate between the entertainment known for card tricks and cabinet illusions (magic) and techniques for harnessing internal and external energies that will help us change ourselves and our environment (magick). Magick is neutral, neither good nor evil. The practitioner decides how they would like to use and focus this natural energy.

So what place does the unicorn have in magick? In most cases we are first introduced to the image of a unicorn in childhood. This way they represent not merely innocence, but playfulness and a carefree time. As one grows older, that sense of joy and happiness can become tinged with melancholy. It can even become an escape from the potential distressing events of growing up. So in magick, one instils the association to the unicorn with imagination, purity and a free spirit. In short, the goal is to make the unicorn a symbol for hope and possibility. To imbue us with the lively and energetic qualities of vitality and joy as well as help us learn patience and ultimately gain wisdom.

The unicorn and wand are similar iconic references and not only is their shape the defining factor but of both having magical properties. It was with this in mind that in the Anne Stokes "Legends" tarot deck she dedicated a whole suit to the unicorn; the wands. As well as using it to represent the major arcane card, 'The Sun', which her description reads; "The moon gives way to the Sun and with it hope for a better day. And in this new day lies a new start; an opportunity to see more clearly and take pleasure in the things that were hidden". The Sun represents the peace of mind in tarot. Anne frequently depicts a glow at the end of her unicorn's horn in her art. It is her way of pictorially depicting the magick within the animal.

Recently in the J K Rowling's Harry Potter™ series of books, unicorn hair can be used in making wands as they produce the most consistent magic. Apparently, they are less prone to magical fluctuations thus making them one of the most faithful of wands. They do not however make the most powerful of wands and the wielder is prone to melancholy if mishandled.

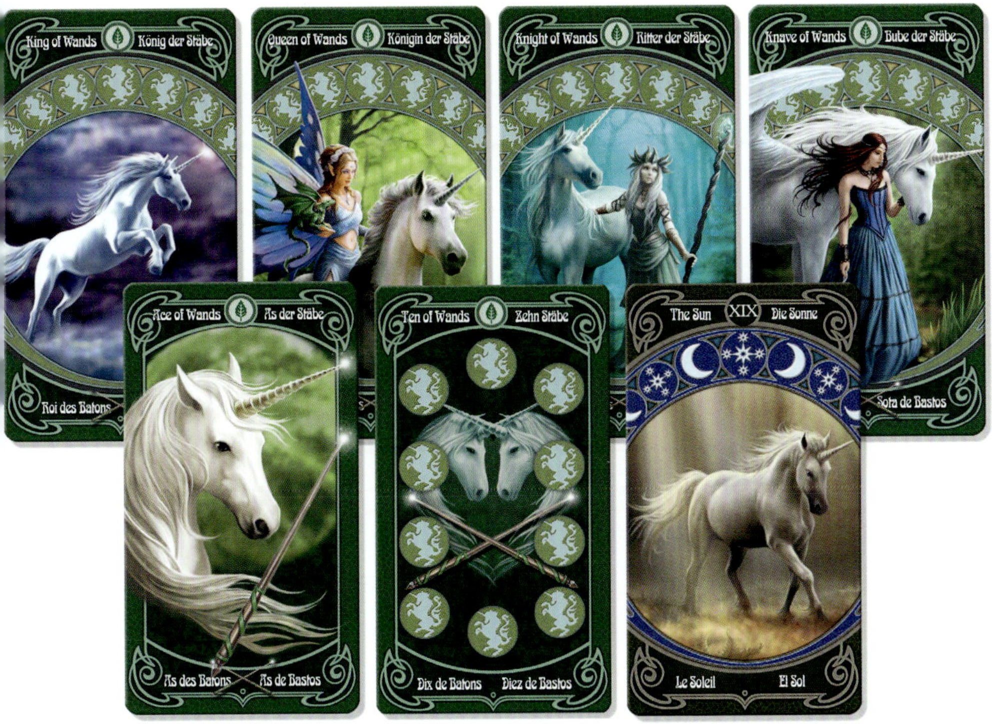

In modern pop culture and media, emphasis has been placed on the association between unicorns and rainbows. Although not as rare as the sighting of a unicorn, the appearance of a rainbow is often viewed with awe and thought to bring both joy and luck. We relate unicorns and rainbows to describe what it means to finally find a true happy ending, the combination of two beautiful things. Could be that when you find your unicorn it may possibly lead you to the end of the rainbow and to that proverbial pot-of-gold.

Since the times of the ancient Greeks, the unicorn has been a part of spell-casting. Always represented likewise as a benevolent and spiritual creature, the unicorn spells are utilized to enhance karma and inner peace. The use of natural items allows the spirit to reconnect with the hidden elements that surround us all. Elements and powers that we have ceased to be aware of, and yet, are still at work guiding our destinies.

Crystal Empowerment Spell

For the following spell you will need:

- A piece of Quartz crystal
- Salt
- A length of wood
- Ribbon

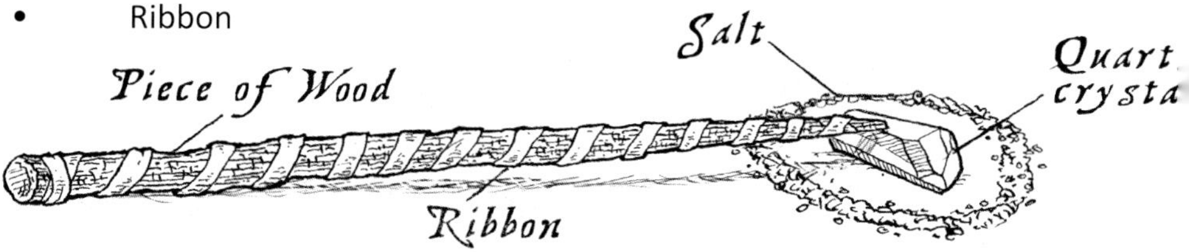

Quartz is a clear or white form of silicone dioxide found throughout the world. Its powers in Magick have been used by shamans and healers for thousands of years. It is also known in practice as 'The Witch's Mirror' and 'Star Stone'. Quartz crystal absorbs energy from the Sun and draws in the life force that lies within trees and plant life.

Salt is used for purification. It was an important commodity in the ancient world and remains so today. The best type of salt to use for magick is either sea salt or kosher salt. Whereas table salt often has iodine added and is considered contaminated for the purpose of spell-casting.

As for your piece of wood that will represent both the unicorn horn and become a basis for a wand? Although without getting too deep into the actual making of a 'true' wand, and the whole what-and-what-not wood to use, there are some points to follow. The length needs to approximate the distance between the tips of your fingers to your elbow. Ideally as straight as possible as the energy needs to flow rather than meander. The base needs to be no thicker than the circumference of your index finger and taper out towards the end. As examples; Willow, Mulberry, Ash or Rowan are known to be excellent for wand woods.

Finally, our ribbon represents the spiralling of the unicorn horn. The clockwise spiralling we are creating on the wand channels the power of the spiral. It helps energy to flow smoothly; as opposed to anti-clockwise which denotes the inability of energy to flow. It is also related to the Golden Ratio Spiral which is found in nature as the Fibonacci sequence; possibly the most simple recurrence relation occurring in nature that we know of.

The following spell needs to be performed on the first day in which a full-moon will fall.

Take your piece of wood and secure the ribbon at the base. Holding it at its base, begin to rotate it clockwise through your fingers and drawing the ribbon out allow it to spiral towards the end. Once there, again, secure it firstly making sure it is quite taut to the wand.

The next step is to find a place that is exposed to sunlight for more than three hours; a windowsill is ideal.

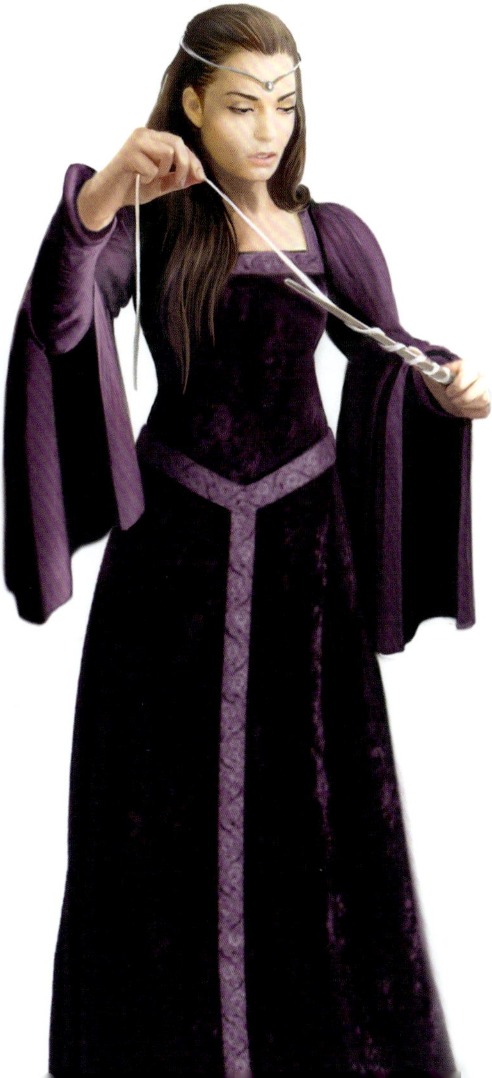

On the morning of the first day of a full-moon, create a ring of salt and place the quartz crystal at its centre. Now take your wand and lay it down so the tip rests upon the crystal, making sure you do not break the circle of salt. Leave for 24 hours and the crystal will absorb both the energy of the sun and moon, as well as empowering the wand with the spirit of the unicorn.

The crystal can now be removed from the ring of salt (which should be scattered outside your front door to protect) and carried with you. At any time you can draw from that energy within the crystal when needed, as it will boost the positive vibrations found within your own chakra. As for the wand; store this safely within your bedroom for the spirit of the unicorn now resides within it. You should find that your sleep is more restful, your dreams unencumbered by nightmares and awake feeling positive. Repeat the spell at the next full-moon to 'recharge' your crystal.

The Black Unicorn

A creature filled with magick energy is the Black Unicorn. This inherits a more macabre pedigree than the white. In some cultures it is seen as an omen of bad luck. If on a dark, cold night one were to see it rearing and hear the scream of its awful equine call, it is said to herald the death of a loved one.

In Scottish folklore it is believed to be associated with the fabled Kelpie, a shape-shifting water spirit inhabiting the lochs and pools of Scotland. Stories of such malevolent water spirits served the practical purpose of keeping children away from perilous areas of water. When a kelpie appeared in its equine persona without any tack, it could be captured using a halter marked with the sign of a cross, its strength could then be harnessed in heavy tasks; such as the transportation of mill stones.

As with faerie mythology, no unicorn can withstand the pain of being shackled with chains of iron. But the black unicorn if successfully chained in these would ignite and turn into a fiery-ash. Then, if shovelled up with an iron spade and put into a hearth the fire shall burn and never go out, until sprinkled with holy water.

In some Eastern cultures it is called the 'Bringer of the Dawn', and is thought to be a servant of Chang-O, Chinese Goddess of the Moon. It is written to have been assigned by her with the duty of chasing away the night ahead of the sun.

Awake the Dawn

The darkness and solitude of night ceases to be,
for with ancient magic the slumbering spell of
night has been broken. The black stallion rears
aloft to greet the new dawn and with it hope for
a brighter tomorrow. Forever shall we be grateful
and give thanks to this symbol of hope.

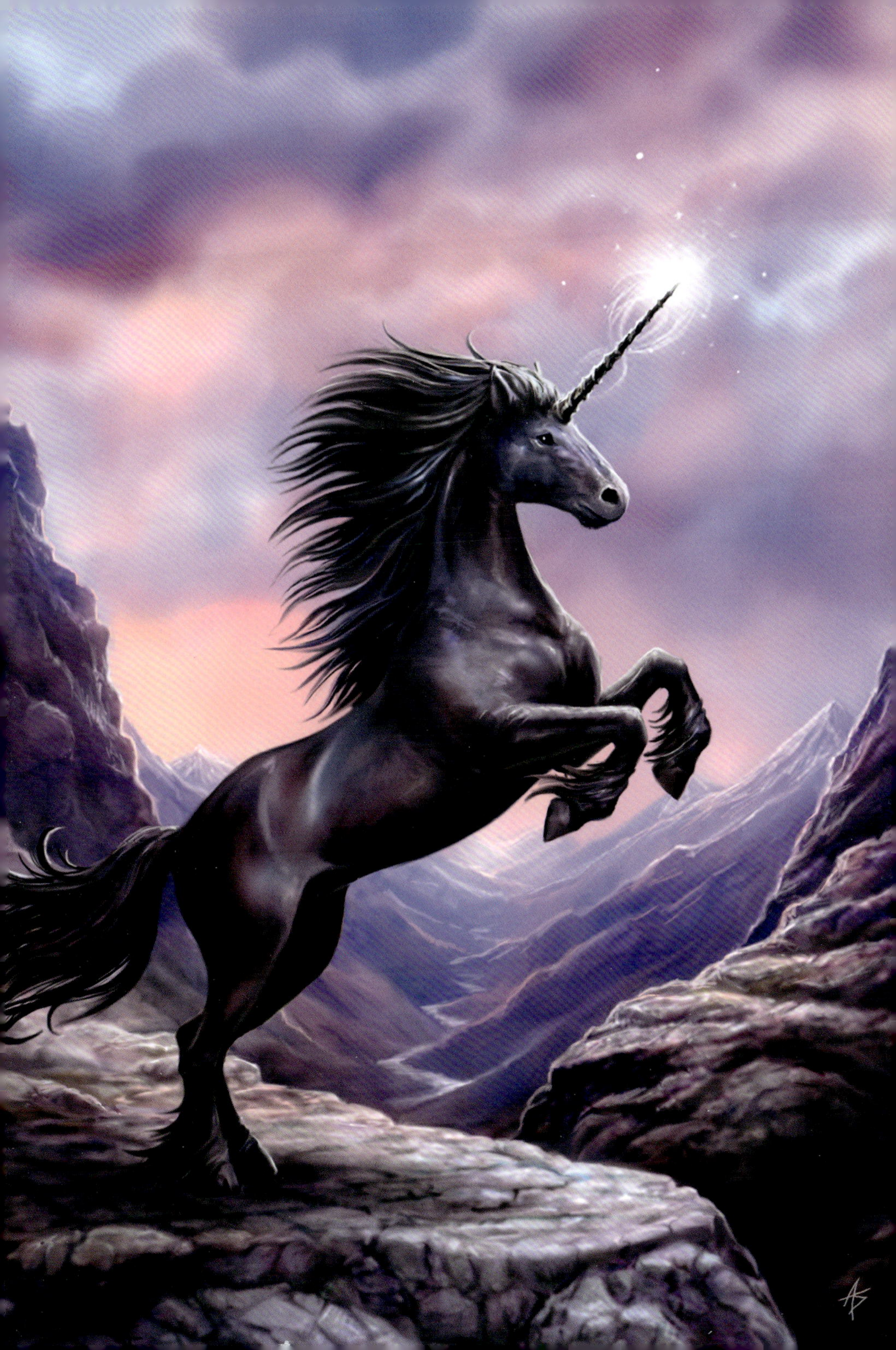

Throughout written history it isn't only the unicorns which possess magical properties. Equine elements have also been the major features of the following:

Pegasus: Without a doubt, Pegasus is one of the most well known creatures of Greek mythology. It is said that he sprang from the blood of the gorgon Medusa's head after being severed by Perseus. During the Middle Ages, Pegasus was the symbol of wisdom and his image has continued to this day as one of speed and bravery.

Hippocampus: Hippocampus is depicted as having the upper body of a horse with the lower body of a fish. Closely related to the hippocampus is the "sea goat", represented by the astrological sign of Capricorn. As magical creatures, it was their duty to draw Poseidon's chariot through the sea.

Sleipnir: In Norse mythology, Sleipnir is an eight-legged horse and was ridden by Odin. Being a magical beast it was able to travel, with Odin, to Helheim (the hidden realm) the underworld in which the dead resided.

Hippogryph: The hippogryph is a creature of legend which has the front half of an eagle and the hind half of a horse. It is said to be extremely fast and able to fly around the world and to the Moon. It was ridden by magicians and was another favourite subject matter used in heraldry.

Pegacorn: A winged unicorn is a magical creature combining the wings of Pegasus and the horn of a unicorn. Such an animal has no specific name, but in some literature, art and media it has been referred to as pegacorn or an alicorn (a term also used to refer to the horn of a unicorn). And it is said that it can only be ridden by a courageous hero or dark sorceress.

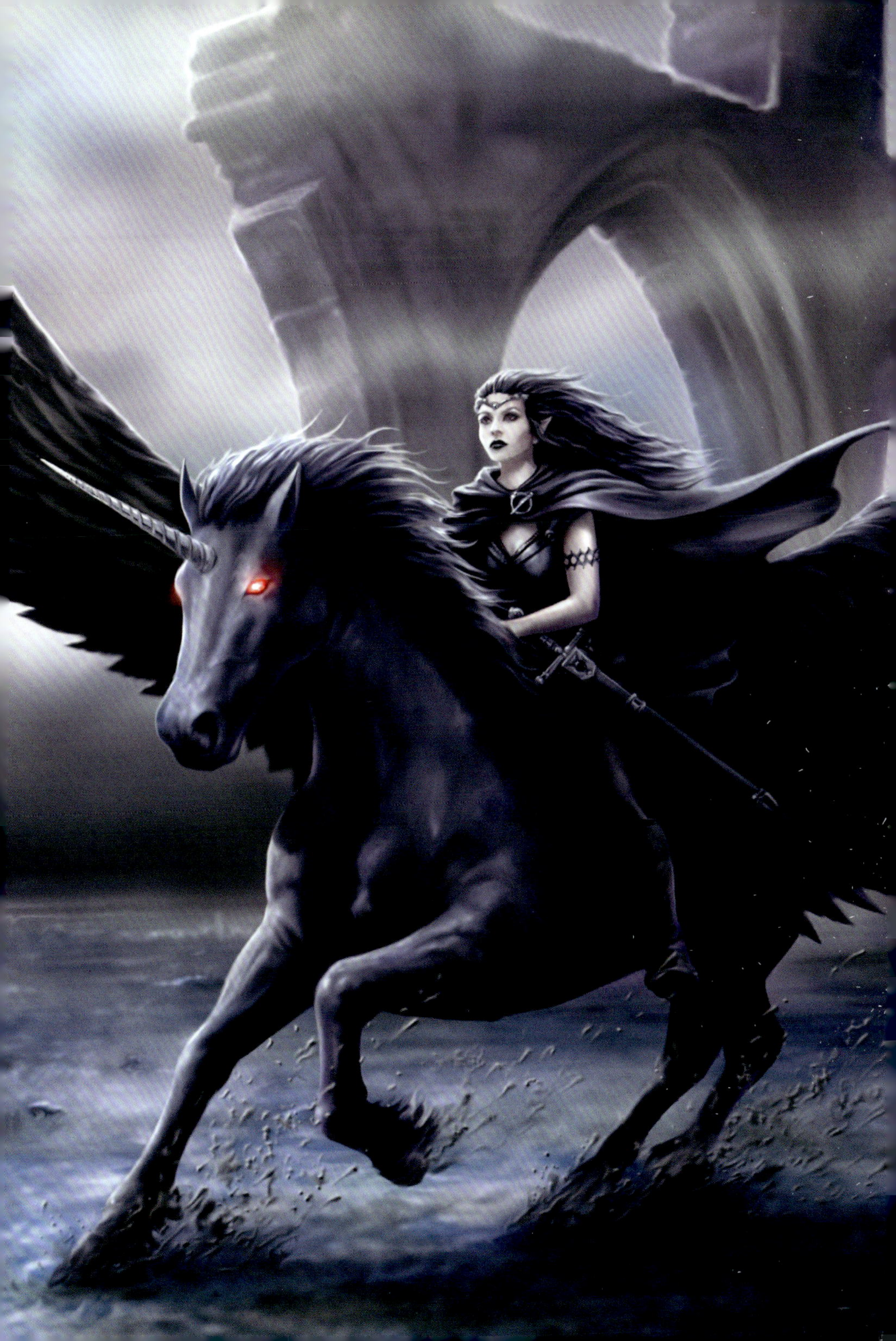

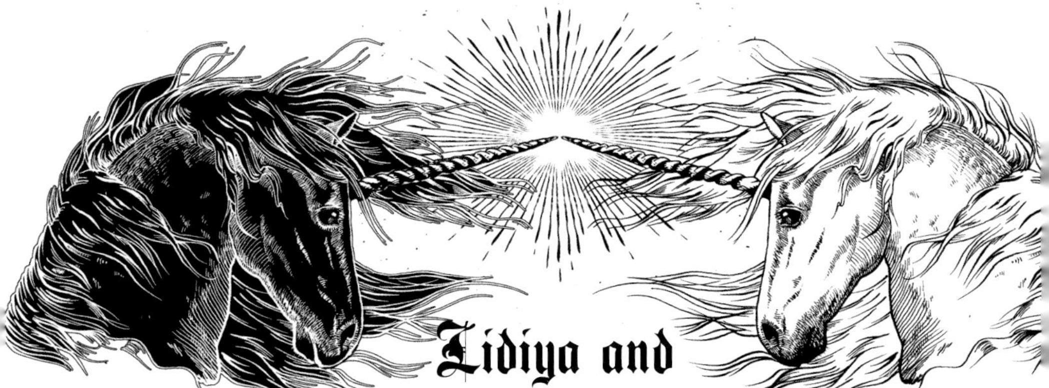

Lidiya and the Black Unicorn

Story by John Woodward

Here is a tale to tell of a black unicorn that was said to be so evil it left pestilence, carnage and death in its wake. Where it came from no one knew although many believed it came from the very depths of hell itself. Tales of it had been told by travellers for countless years, which in turn had become stories told to children at night to scare them into being good.
"Mind yourselves little ones, or the Black Unicorn will steal you away." Babushkas would say.

Long ago, in the small village of Utaya, Russia lived a little girl Lidiya and her younger brother Georgy. Their father was the blacksmith and a well respected man within the community. For being so far from the nearest town of Zyryanka which was just over 100 miles away, horses were essential to the villagers.

It was October and the first snow had begun to softly fall. It was late in the day and the lanterns were being lit in the windows of the cabins. Lidiya was the first to hear it, faint at first and then rhythmically getting louder. She ran inside to her Father.

"Papa, do you hear it? What is it?" she asked curiously.
Her father straightened from his chores, laid the hammer onto the anvil and walked past the young girl to the open door. He stepped out and joined the others drawn by the sound.

"Stepan, you hear"? said someone.
He listened attentively, turning his head slowly to assess the direction. "It's horses...maybe six or eight." The blacksmith replied. "And they are riding as if the devil himself were chasing them." he added. Some of the men went back inside and returned brandishing scimitars, sickles and other objects

that could be used as a weapon of defence. The women ushered the children inside and stood in their doorways. Anticipation was high.

In a short while into the centre of the village rode eight unarmed riders, the steam rising from the sweat on their horses. The riders breathless also, one by one they dismounted and resting their arms on their knees gulped in huge breaths of air. The blacksmith gestured to the villagers that action wouldn't be required.

"Gentlemen, come into my workshop for my forge is hot and I have ale." he offered.

They dismounted and one by one followed him into the workshop; the villagers followed too and huddled around the open barn door. After the blacksmith had duly issued each of the men a tankard of ale, he asked.

"Where are you travelling to in such haste"? Adding "Your horses can travel no further without good rest, I can tell you that".

The men all looked at each other and fear was evident upon their faces. Finally one stepped forward; he stole a glance at the villagers standing grouped in the entrance and then looked directly at the blacksmith.

"The Black Unicorn is coming!" he said.

The riders had come from the west, from a village no larger than Utaya. There the villagers went about their daily routines. Children played, the old folk reminisced how things were better when they were younger and the cries of the market traders made it just another normal day. All that had changed four days ago when the Black Unicorn had appeared. Its arrival had been preceded by dark, foreboding clouds that had blotted out what little sun there was at this time of year. Thunder rumbled and lightening crackled, filling the air with static. Then, as if born from the very black clouds themselves, swarmed flocks of dark birds that swirled maniacally in ever changing formations. It was an apocalyptic sight to behold. The villagers all stood in awe to what was happening around them and their hearts froze as the Black Unicorn came into sight.

The rider who had been recounting his experience stopped; the horror of what he had seen was etched upon his face and he could not continue. It was evident that these eight were now the sole survivors of that village to the West.

"So we have four days until it arrives here, yes?" asked Stepan coolly.

The rider was brought back from his dark thoughts by the question and answered dolefully, "If it follows our trail...which it surely will, then yes, four days".

Several of the women that huddled in the entrance let out cries and sobs. The men muttered deeply under their breaths and clenched their fists.

Lidiya and Georgy sat upon the stairs that led from the workshop to their home above. Both had watched and listened to the events of the evening unfold; first with faces filled with wonder and now replaced by alarm.

"You hear that Sister, the Black Unicorn is coming for us? Georgy said forlornly.

Lidiya put her arms around her brother and rocked him gently, just as her mother had done to her when she was a baby. She thought of her now and of what her father called her, the fairest angel in God's company.

Below, her father addressed the crowd with firmness, saying "Go home and think upon what we should do?" adding, "We all will meet back here in the morning, try and get some sleep".

He knew that the latter was something no one would be getting that night.

Later Lidiya knelt by her bed and placing her hands together closed her eyes in prayer.

"Mama, what shall we do?" she said. "The Black Unicorn is on its way to our village and I'm frightened for Papa and Georgy." She paused as if expecting an answer. Finally she asked, "If there is anything that you can do, Mama, please help us?"

In that moment, high in the clear, cold-pitch-black night sky over the village, one star seemed to flicker brighter than all the rest.

In the morning it was unanimously agreed upon that the village would be abandoned and refuge be sought in the nearby mountains two days walk away. There they would wait for the Black Unicorn to pass through and then, if safe, return home.

"How will we know it is safe to return?" the miller had asked anxiously. Without hesitation, his mind already made on the matter, the blacksmith stepped forward and addressed them all saying, "I alone shall stay behind and when danger has passed I will light a beacon...only then will you return".

The fortitude upon his face was clear to all assembled; they knew it was futile to argue the matter.

After the meeting had dispersed he knelt, he took a hand from each of his children he looked into their tearful eyes, saying, "You will go with Babushka Luda, it is arranged, she will keep you safe". His voice was controlled and firm. "And as you heard me say, once the danger has gone you shall come back to me, alright?" The children said nothing, for they loved and respected their father, both just nodded acceptance of the plan.

Just after midday, taking only what was essential the villagers made a sad spectacle as they all departed reluctantly. The few that looked back saw the blacksmith standing stoically in the village square watching them depart. Babushka Luda huddled the two children to her as she walked. Under her flowing shawl the old woman looked like an owl protecting her young and the blacksmiths heart almost broke. He knew they would be safe.

No time was wasted and he toiled hard and long into that first night. He blocked all main entrances to the village with carts. These were then loaded with straw bales and barrels to give them weight and stability. Next, checking that fires and stoves were extinguished in all the premises was also essential. For, if this plan worked he didn't want accidental fires resulting in no homes for the families to come home to. Only then did he make sure the shutters and doors were all closed.

The horses he corralled in a grazing area a couple of miles away west in the hope they wouldn't take fright and flee for they were essential to the survival of the village. It was past midnight by the time he returned from this last endeavour and collapsed into the hay in the workshop exhausted.

The villagers reached the mountains on the evening of the second day. There they made their way to the caves. These were stocked with adequate quantities of wood, straw and barrels of fresh water; for they also served as refuge during some of the more severe winters.

The following morning found the blacksmith working feverously at his forge. He had piled as much wood as he could near to it so as to never let the fire go out. He had made two large and wieldy swords of iron by using all the old horseshoes. Remembering the old tales of how iron was used to repel evil spirits, fairies and witches. Smelting them and mixing with carbon, he hammered into shape, and then after quenching them in water spent a long time sharpening them. Only when the sun had gone down and he was happy with their edge did he wrap the handles in thick hide. When he'd completed this last task, he laid them down close to the forge and sought the sleep he knew would not come.

On the morning of the fourth day found him atop the church steeple. Although sparse in design it had been lovingly constructed several generations earlier and its rustic exterior hid the gem within. Inside the wooden panels that covered the walls and ceilings had been decorated with icons of such delicacy and beauty that they could do nought but inspire prayer to a divinity.

Adoration was the farthest thing from his mind as he stared out towards the Eastern horizon. His eyes stung from the sleep that had evaded him. But he knew what was at stake here; he rubbed his eyes and shook his head to dispel the tiredness.

Just after midday he saw the horizon darken. From a north easterly direction it came. He fixed his focus on it and watched the darkness grow in intensity, knowing it was getting nearer. The sky changed and it seemed to be a living thing. It swirled, dipped and bobbed in a mesmerizing, yet uncanny, display. Then he realized he was watching countless numbers of dark birds flying in wild ever-changing patterns.

He flew down the ladder and bolted from the church to his workshop. There he plunged the swords into the forge and pumped the bellows with all his might. Sparks flew everywhere and the blacksmith paid no mind to those that settled and singed his skin.

The Black Unicorn shattered the laden carriage as if it were made from matchsticks. It entered the village square, circled several times and then reared on to its hind legs. It let forth a bellow from deep within its throat, a sound so terrible it was unlike anything heard before. In the workshop he stopped bellowing the forge and moving around withdrew the glowing swords from the fire.

As he walked out into the unnatural darkness, he stole a glance upwards and beheld the churning vortex of dark birds he'd witnessed earlier. He looked over to where the Black Unicorn stood and shuddered. It was larger than any horse he had shod. Plumes of breath, like steam, issued from its flaring nostrils and its glowing red eyes were fixed upon him. It truly was a vision spawned of hell.

The blacksmith held the glowing weapons down at arm's length. Then, ran headlong at the hellspawn; as he did, he let forth a cry of fury. His anger was focused wholeheartedly at this thing that dared to walk the earth. That took the souls of countless victims in its wake without remorse. The Black Unicorn reacted likewise and lowering its head charged. At the very last moment the blacksmith arched to one side and avoided being impaled on its horn. In that moment, he drew the sword in his right hand across its shoulder and it cut deep from there to its belly. Its flank caught him a blow and he was knocked spiralling to the ground. Behind him the Black Unicorn screamed. But as the blacksmith rose and turned to face the demon he stared in disbelief as the inflicted wound healed itself before his eyes. He knew in that instance that death had come for him this day.

Without pause the Black Unicorn moved with lightning speed and caught him totally unprepared. He had a fraction of a second to move to his left and in doing so it saved his life. Instead of the horn piercing his heart it gouged deep into his shoulder. The beast tossed him to one side as if he was a mere rag doll.

As he lay there on the ground he became aware of the calls from the flocks swirling above. Almost akin to spectators in a gladiatorial fight baying for the dispatch of the defeated opponent. The wound in his shoulder burned with an intensity he couldn't have imagined; it began to slowly spread over him. The end had surely come.

At that moment silence abruptly fell. The dark birds were quiet and the Black Unicorn stood quite still. The blacksmith looked across at it and was surprised to see that the demon wasn't looking at him; its eyes were fixed on something else. He turned his head in the opposite direction and gave out a sob.

In the middle of the street stood Lidiya and behind her in a light of pure and radiant light stood a large and elegant white unicorn. The Black Unicorn let out another fearful roar and rose repeatedly upon its hind legs whilst raking the air with its front hooves in seeming protest.

Lidiya moved to one side as if commanded to do so and the white unicorn moved majestically past her. Only then did she run over to where her father lay. She knelt by his side and flung her arms over him avoiding the wound in his shoulder. She kissed his cheek and said,
"Look Papa, Mama has sent us an angel".

The two unicorns came together in battle and the world shook. On and on they fought with limitless energy and each receiving terrible wounds from the other. The blacksmith noted that this time the Black Unicorn's injuries did not heal themselves. All the while Lidiya clung to her Father.

A vicious blow caught the white unicorn and it fell awkwardly backwards to the ground. Sensing victory the Black Unicorn reared up ready to plunge the horn into the defenceless opponent. In that split second, the white unicorn pushed itself up and with the last ounce of strength pierced the Black Unicorn's heart. Its eyes widened and the glowing red light within faded. It toppled sideways dead.

A grey misty light began to replace the darkness and small flakes of snow began to fall gently. The dark birds had vanished; the black clouds were dispersing like drops of ink swirled in water. Only then did Lidiya let go her father and stand. She looked across at the fallen demon and slowly it began to crumble into ash and was no more. The breeze swept it up and scattered it away.

The white unicorn rose and walked wearily across to where the blacksmith lay. It bowed its head and a single tear fell from its eye upon injured man's shoulder. He winced and drew in a deep breath, he felt the healing warmth coursing though his body and he smiled up at the unicorn. As he did he felt a pang of recognition? Lidiya reached up and stroking the saviour said simply and softly, "Thank you".

She felt her father's strong arms and she turned and fell into his embrace. They stayed like that for some time and after she had helped him to his feet they both stood and looked around. The white unicorn was nowhere to be seen.

That evening the villagers rejoiced as they saw the flames from the bonfire reach into the night sky. They gathered their belongings ready for their journey home.

The End

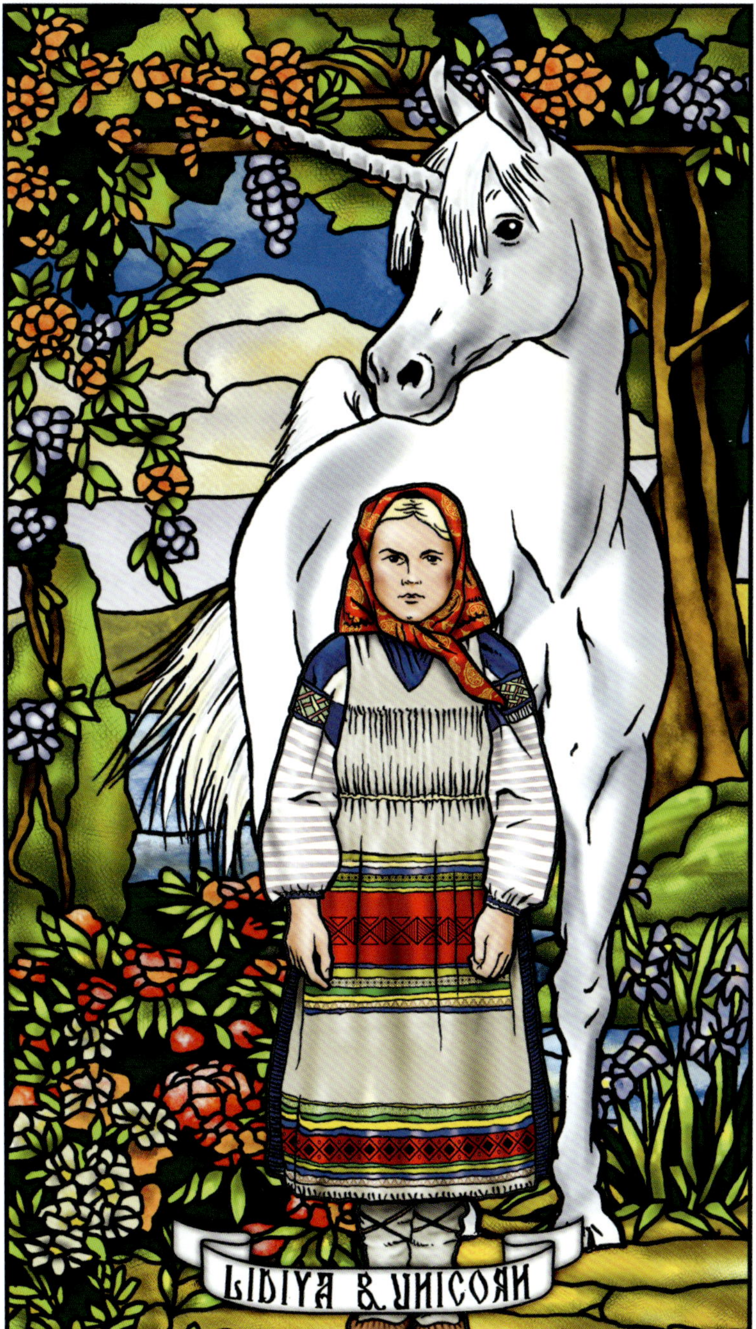
LIDIYA & UNICORN
JWI

"...if you'll believe in me, I'll believe in you. Is that a bargain?"

CHAPTER VIII

Literature

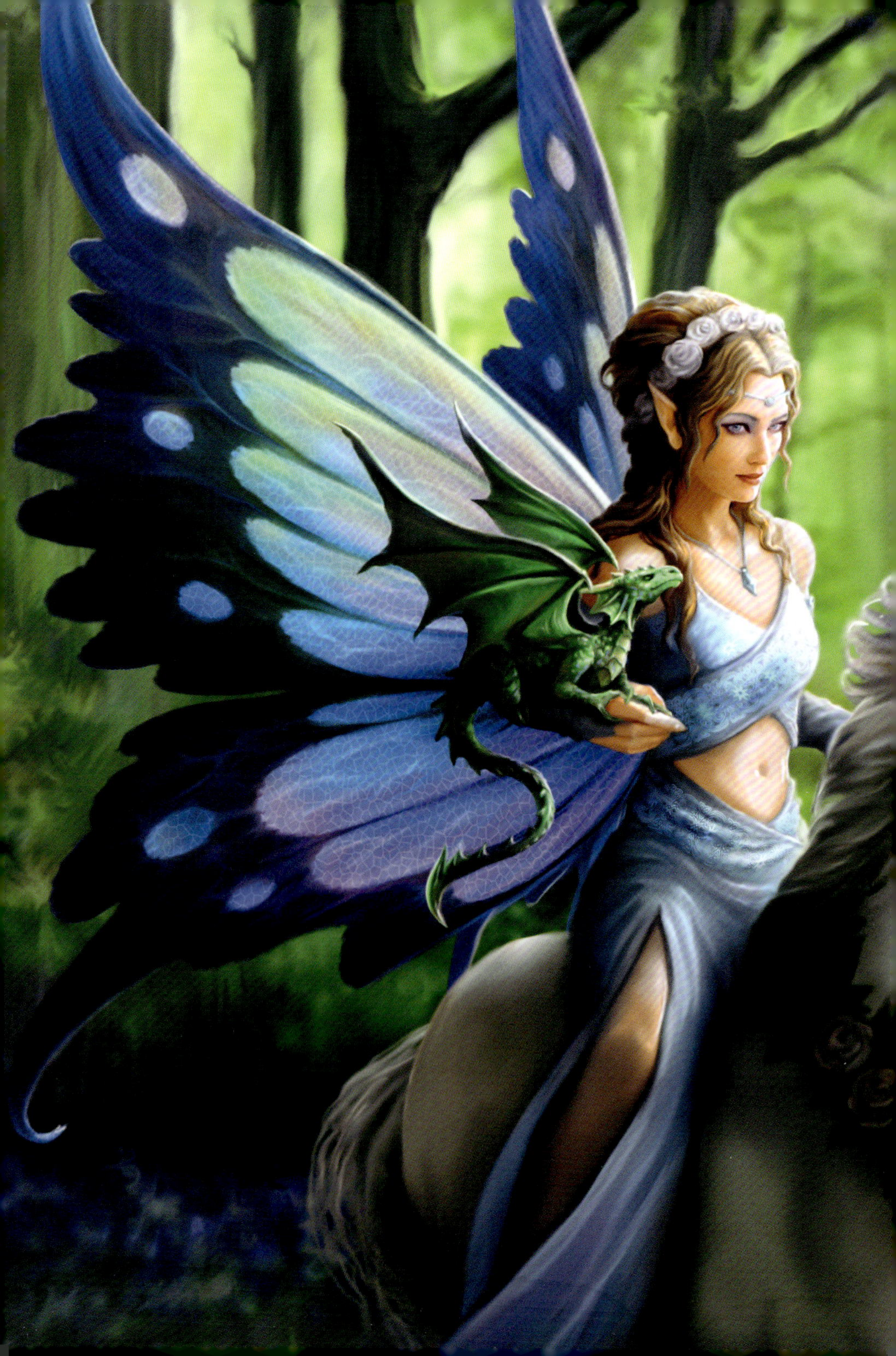

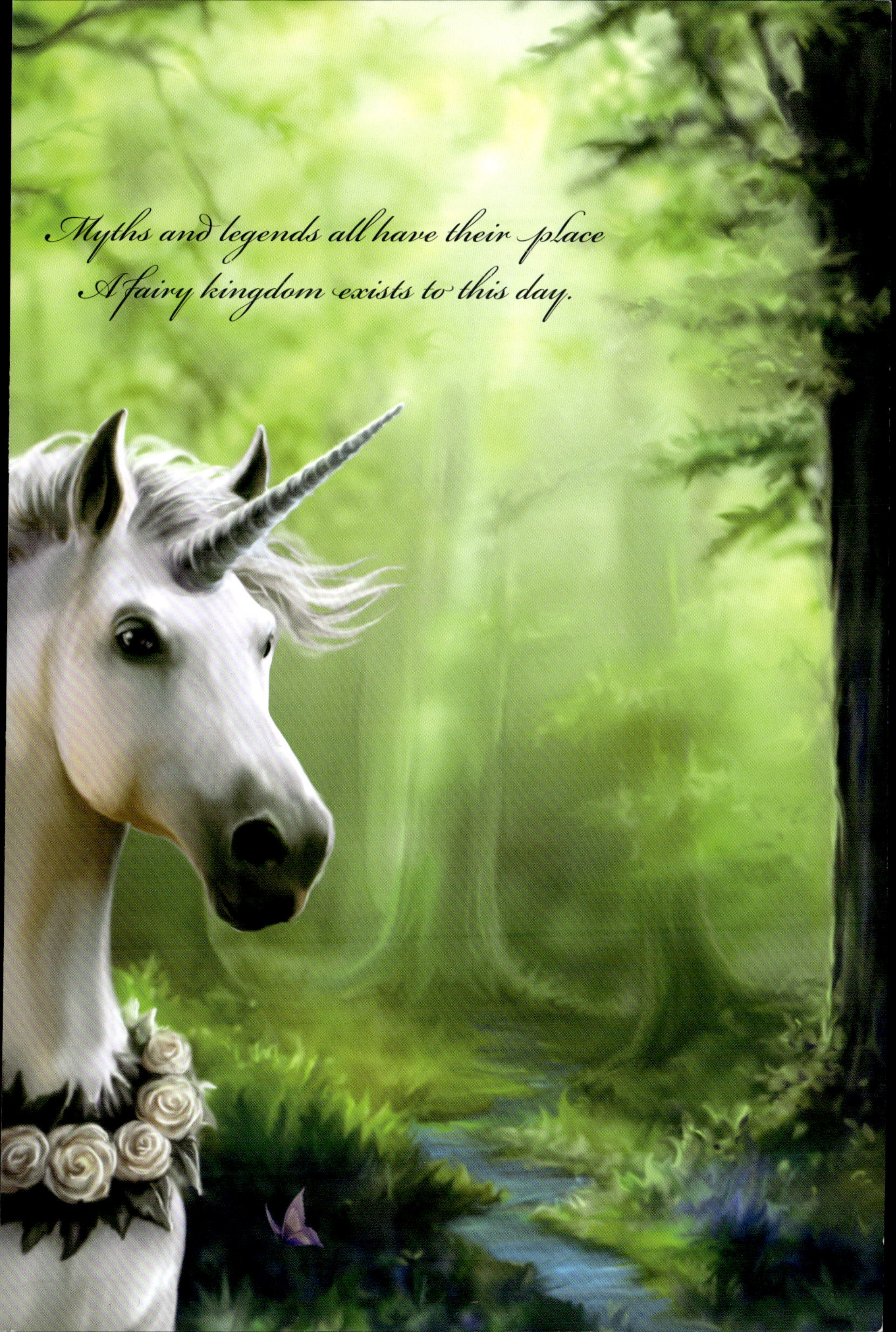
Myths and legends all have their place
A fairy kingdom exists to this day.

Since man found a language with which to convey his thoughts and emotions, tales of the unicorn have been told. In song, sonnets, poems, plays and novels they have all aided in belief. Aside from the previously mentioned King James Bible the unicorn has been the perfect metaphor for truth and beauty in literature as well as all things mystical and unexplained.

I myself as a child was captivated by the stories of **C.S.Lewis** (1898-1963), especially the Chronicles of Narnia series of books. I well remember to this day Jewel the Unicorn aide and friend to Tirian, King of Narnia and the part he played in 'The Last Battle'.

Another, 'The Last Unicorn', is a wonderful and enchanting fantasy novel by **Peter S. Beagle** (b.1939). The tale of a unicorn, who believes she is the last of her kind in the world and undertakes a quest to discover what has happened to the others. It was also made into an animated movie with an all-star voice cast, also worth seeking out.

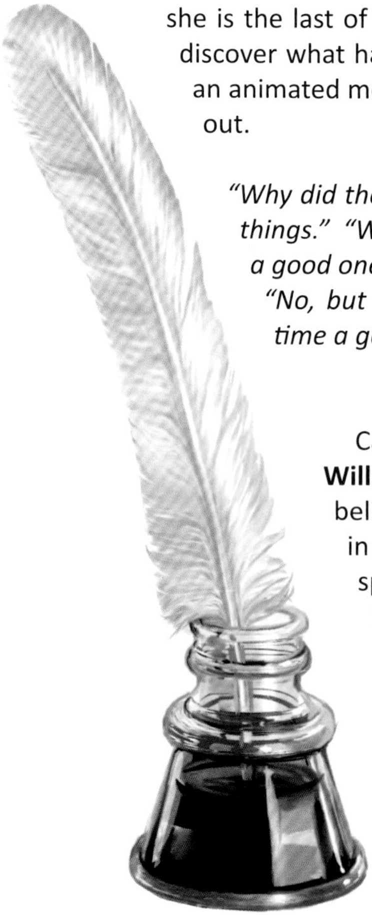

"Why did they go away, do you think? If there ever were such things." "Who knows? Times change. Would you call this age a good one for unicorns?"
"No, but I wonder if any man before us ever thought his time a good time for unicorns."

- The Last Unicorn

Can it be said of England's most famous playwright, **William Shakespeare** (1564–1616), whether he believed in unicorns? It's true that the animal features in several of his plays although he writes for the speakers to talk in disbelief. I personally think that it's safe to infer that he didn't believe in unicorns. Which is an extraordinary thought, considering many of his contemporaries accepted the existence of such without question. In a way he believed, albeit imaginatively, in the same way he needed to believe in writing about ghosts, fairies, witches etc.

"Now I will believe that there are unicorns..."
William Shakespeare, The Tempest

Charles Lutwidge Dodgson (1832-1898), better known by his pen-name **Lewis Carroll** wrote in 'Through the Looking Glass, and What Alice Found There' (1871) a wonderful topsy-turvy account of the heroine coming upon the Lion and the Unicorn from the old nursery rhyme. Again, both are fighting over the crown which now belongs to the White King; however, as they both serve the same monarch it makes the squabble absurd. Upon breaking up the fight the unicorn mistakes Alice as a mythical monster but finally resolving the mistake, says to Alice, "...if you'll believe in me, I'll believe in you. Is that a bargain?"

In modern literature, for instance, the unicorn is mentioned several times throughout the hugely successful Harry Potter series of novels, written by **J.K.Rowling** (b.1965). In the debut book, 'Harry Potter and the Philosopher's Stone', unicorns are slain by the antagonist to aid their return to power by killing them and drinking their blood.

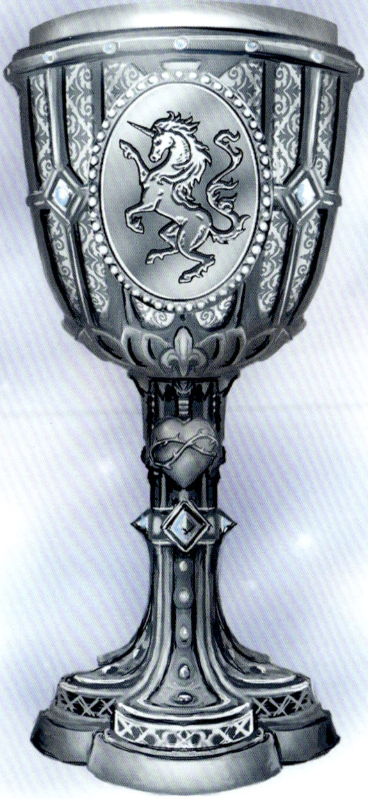

"Only one who has nothing to lose, and everything to gain, would commit such a crime. The blood of a unicorn will keep you alive, even if you are an inch from death, but at a terrible price. You have slain something pure and defenceless to save yourself, and you will have but a half-life, a cursed life, from the moment the blood touches your lips."

- J.K. Rowling, Harry Potter and the Sorcerer's Stone

In **Tennessee Williams** (1911 – 1983)' The Glass Menagerie', a glass unicorn is used to symbolize that the girl was "different to other horses". The horn on this unicorn represented her physical handicap, which prevented her from meeting people. When she finally did meet a man, they danced and knocked over the unicorn, breaking its horn off. "It's just like all the other horses now" she said which symbolizes that she has overcome her shyness and lost her virginity.

Poets too have drawn inspiration through it, John Keats, Robert Graves and Dylan Thomas included. Or the following, written by **Rainer Maria Rilke** (1875-1926), a bohemian-Austrian poet and novelist, who wrote the following, simply titled 'The Unicorn':

The saintly hermit, midway through his prayers
stopped suddenly, and raised his eyes to witness
the unbelievable: for there before him stood
the legendary creature, startling white, that
had approached, soundlessly, pleading with his eyes.

The legs, so delicately shaped, balanced a
body wrought of finest ivory. And as
he moved, his coat shone like reflected moonlight.
High on his forehead rose the magic horn, the sign
of his uniqueness: a tower held upright
by his alert, yet gentle, timid gait.

The mouth of softest tints of rose and grey, when
opened slightly, revealed his gleaming teeth,
whiter than snow. The nostrils quivered faintly:
he sought to quench his thirst, to rest and find repose.
His eyes looked far beyond the saint's enclosure,
reflecting vistas and events long vanished,
and closed the circle of this ancient mystic legend."

The British film director, **Ridley Scott**, uses the unicorn as metaphors in two of his films; Legend (1985), in which the Lord of Darkness seeks to possess the horn of a unicorn, guardians of the Power of Light. And in the director's cut of the movie 'Blade Runner' (1992), the unicorn is used to great symbolic effect. The principal character, Rick Deckard, has a dream featuring the animal. The meaning of the dream is central to his self-identity.

It is clear that literature and media holds a beholden thanks to the history of this remarkable animal. I'm certain that at some point we have all read, heard or seen something that sparked our imagination featuring the unicorn. There are countless more accounts that only go to strengthen the fact that literature would indeed, be a far less interesting subject without them in it.

We couldn't end the literature section without mentioning the great fantasy author **Terry Pratchett** (1948-2015) and some of the wonderful humour in his Discworld series. Here one of his best known characters, the witch Granny Weatherwax says it like it is about the unicorn:

"I thought unicorns were more ... fluffy."

"See clear! Don't let the glamour get you! See what's in front of your eyes! It's a damn great horse with a horn on the end!" said Granny."

- Terry Pratchett, Lords and Ladies

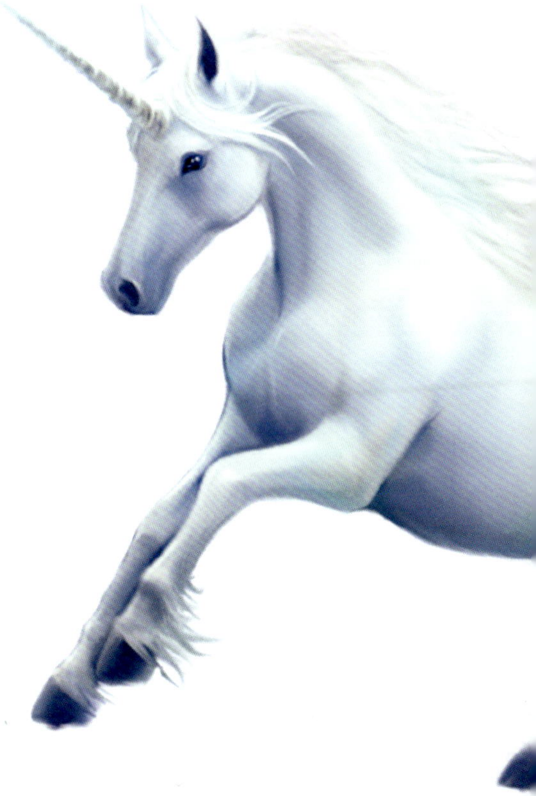

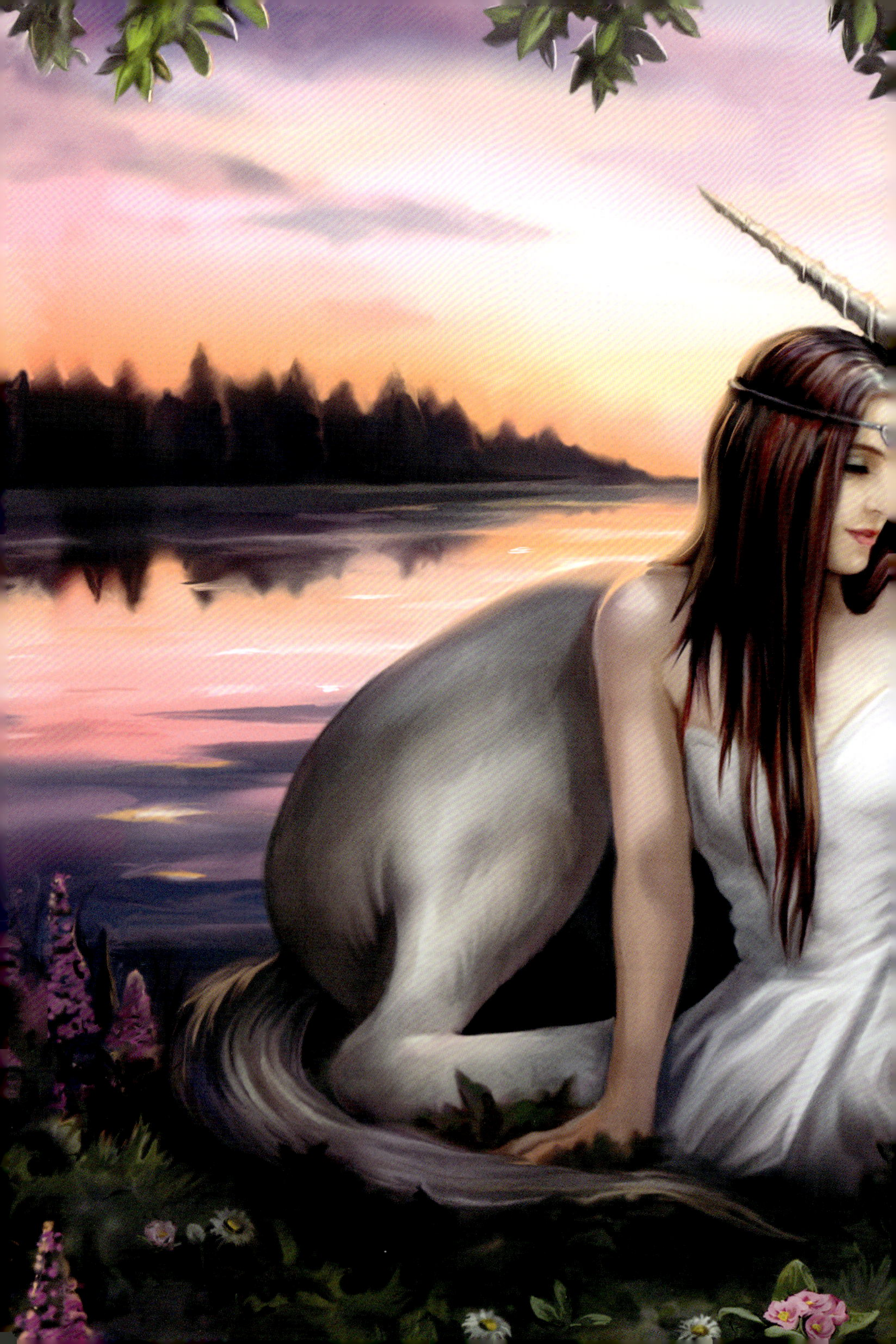

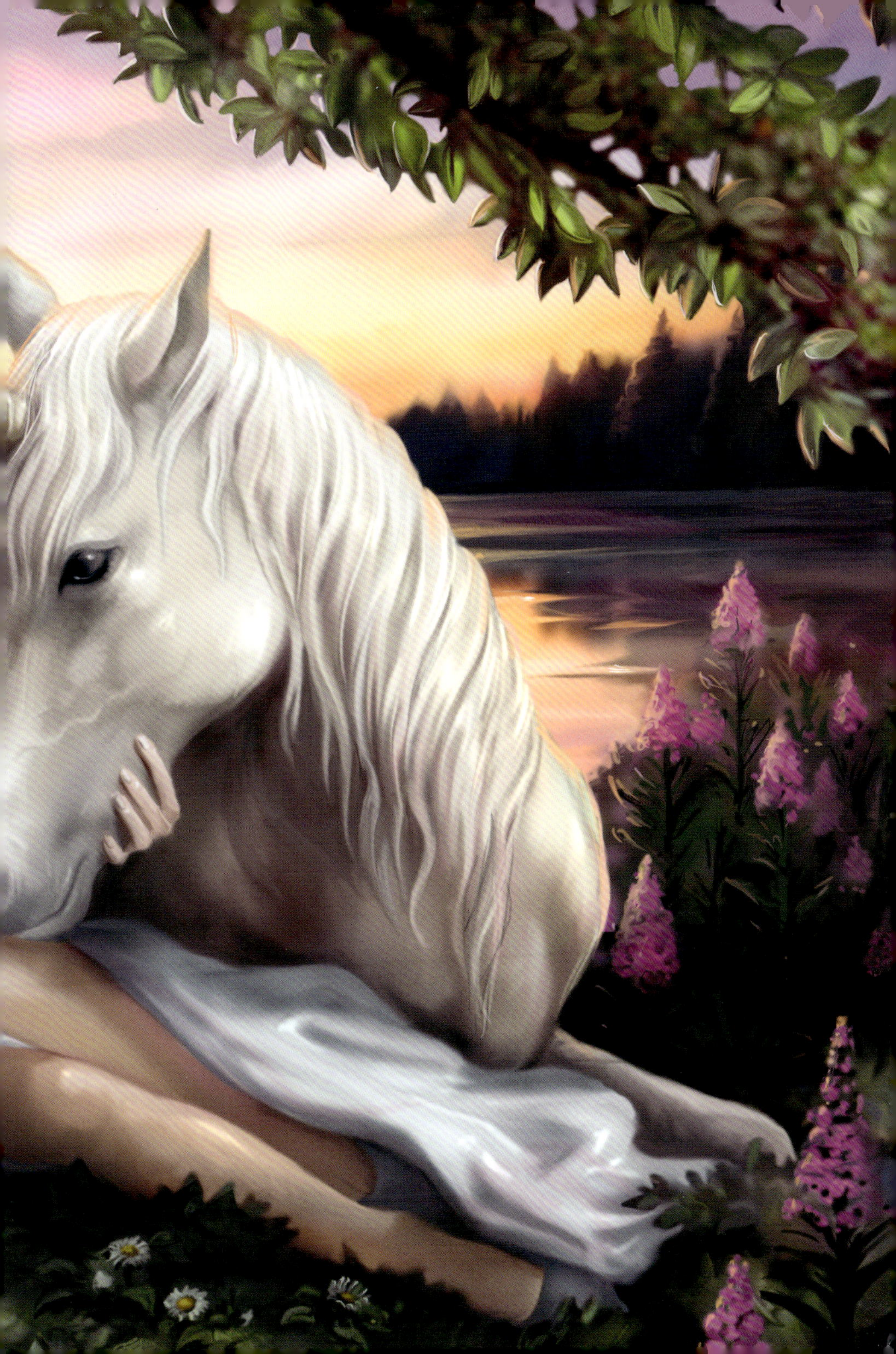

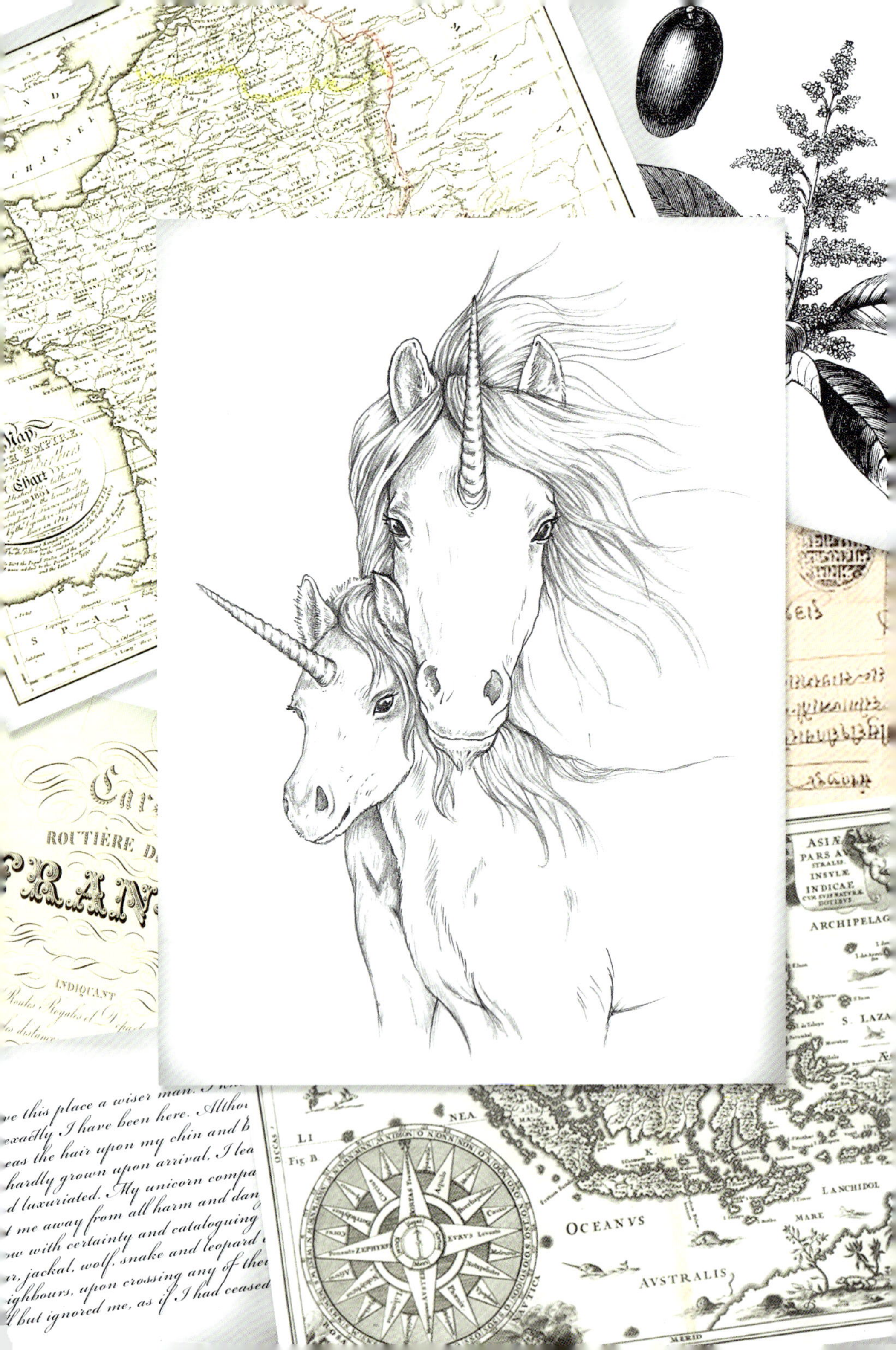
ROUTIÈRE D
INDIQUANT
ASIÆ
PARS AV
STRALIS
INSULÆ
INDICAE
ARCHIPELAG
S. LAZA
LANCHIDOL
MARE
OCEANVS
AUSTRALIS
ve this place a wiser man.
exactly I have been here. Altho
eas the hair upon my chin and
hardly grown upon arrival, I lea
d luxuriated. My unicorn compa
t me away from all harm and dan
w with certainty and cataloguing
r, jackal, wolf, snake and leopard
ighbours, upon crossing any of the
ll but ignored me, as if I had ceased

Throughout history there have been documentation, reports and stories presented as true facts. Yet without true evidence we are sceptical for that is human nature. In the essence of those citations, I hereby add my own tale of what could have been submitted to the academia of old, entitled...

An Encounter in India

Story by John Woodward

In 1792 René Faire-Croire, then only 19, signed aboard the Jardinière as assistant to the botanist Franz Bredemeyer (1758-1839), under Captain Nicolas Baudin (1754-1803) in an expedition to the Indian Ocean and China. The ship departed from the Spanish port of Málaga on 1 October 1792. From the Cape of Good Hope she sailed across the Indian Ocean to the coast of New Holland (Australia), but two consecutive cyclones prevented the expedition from doing any work there and forced Baudin to take the ship to Bombay for repairs.

So it was here that Faire-Croire took his leave and started to explore the interior of India. Much is written before regarding geography and study of the populous of the regions he travelled through. It is the subsequent texts we focus for this inclusion [translated from French]:

"It was now many months since departing my fellow crew and whereas my initial thrill and vigour at being in such an exotic land was very high indeed. I must confess that it had waned to such a point I saw no future and thought me lost forever.

That was until I came upon a place of such breathtaking beauty and wonder that I thought myself to be the only man to have found such peace. Apart from several temples I passed the area I find myself seems quite deserted of human life. I have made shelter and a base camp within a cave which to explore from and return to nightly near to a magnificent waterfall [editor-Sita Khori; in an area we now know to be Gautala Autramghat Sanctuary, Western Ghats].

Several days later, whilst documenting new fauna I was set upon and injured unexpectedly by, what I know today to have been, a leopard. I fought back as one possessed. To this day I know not why, in what would have been its triumph and my departure of this world the beast simply turned and walked away. My left leg had been mauled so savagely that I dared not think of the consequences. For several hours and with the aid of a makeshift crutch I did indeed manage to return to camp. However my cave, accessible only by a short climb, meant that in such a state as I was may have well as been atop Kilimanjaro. Night was drawing in and as I lay my injured leg into the cool waters of the pool below the waterfall I knew that with the darkness came the night hunters. I subsequently drifted in and out of consciousness until I suddenly became are of the approaching light. My fevered thoughts were of natives nearby, having heard my cries of pain and entreaties to the heavens arriving to my aid.

The white light grew brighter by intensity until it seemed to cast away the darkness. So bright and yet I had no need to shield my eyes, there into the light approached a gleaming and wondrous vision of the fabled unicorn. With head held high its spiralling horn seemed to pierce the very sky and then it lowered its gaze and met mine. In that moment my mind became free of all thoughts of pain and distress. Calmness unlike any emotion one could imagine overcame me and in that moment I felt as one with universe. It then dropped its head until the tip of its horn touched the water. In that moment my whole body felt a sensation of both heat and cold. A sensation similar to tingling began to take me over at that point. I presume my body could no longer comprehend what was happening for I lost all consciousness.

When I awoke the sun was high in the clear blue sky and I was alone. I remembered my injury, all though there was no pain to remind me, and looked down at my leg. Through the tatters of my trousers my leg bore neither scratch nor bite".

Later in the journal, after several months have passed, he writes:

"Today I was able to witness a sight I am certain unseen by anyone before. I saw a unicorn being born, whether into this world or another. For as I have previously written that when the unicorn and its mate have visited me on many occasions time itself stops. All sounds, awareness and

reality of this planet are gone, to be replaced with pure peace. To this place unicorn foal was given life.

It is born gold and not the whitest of white as its parents are. It is not ochre, goldenrod or honey by definition, but pure gold and its brilliance is unmatched by nature. I watched as the mother and father touched horns together and seemingly blessed their offspring by placing both upon its forehead. The next time I saw all three together the colt had lost its golden colour and was as radiant as the proud parents by its side."

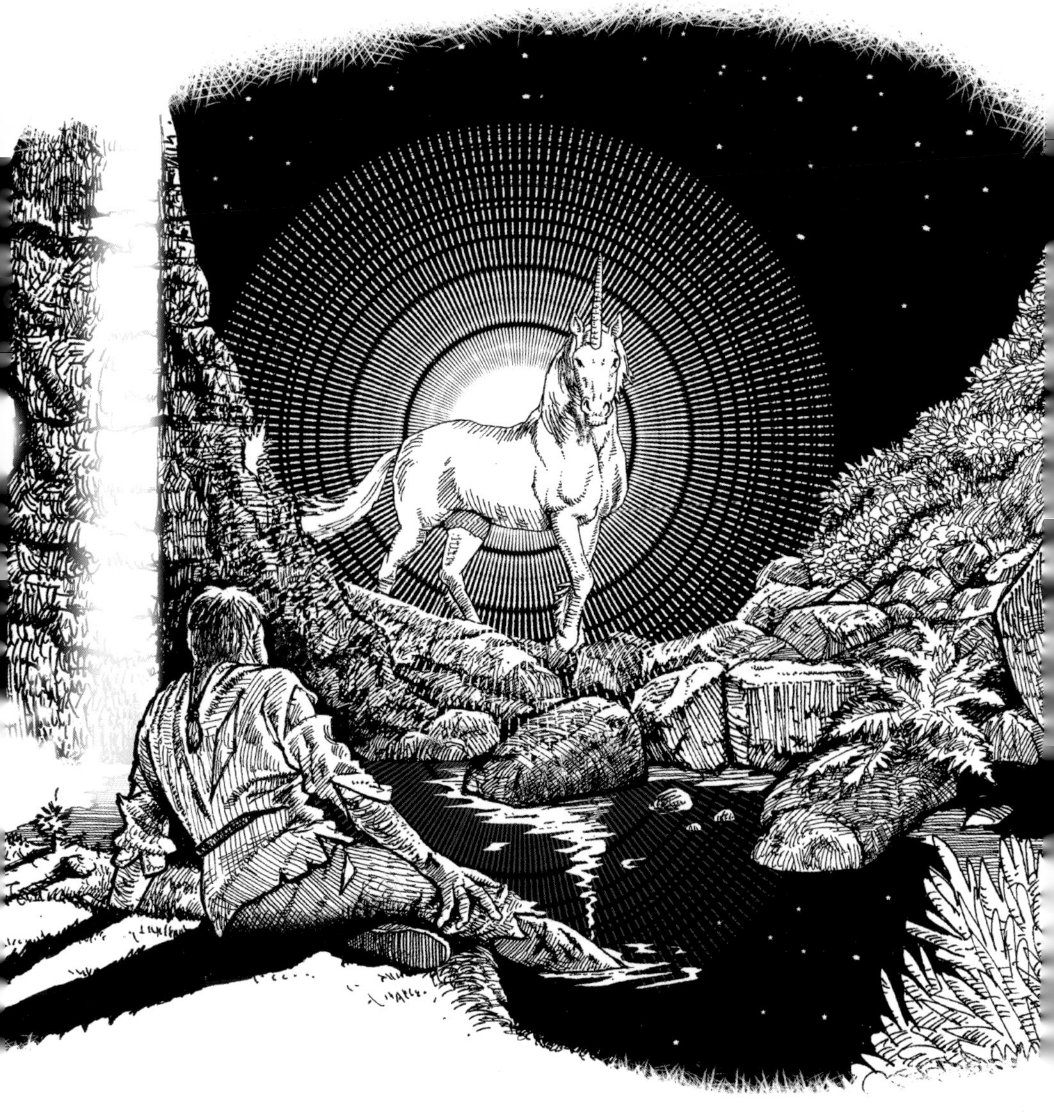

At this point in the journal several pages are missing, clearly ripped out. Speculation ensues as to whether Faire-Croire either regretted what he'd written upon those omitted pages or indeed felt that there was too much personal information. We shall never know. He concludes with the following:

"I leave this place a wiser man. I know not how long exactly I have been here. Although I know whereas the hair upon my chin and body was soft and hardly grown upon arrival, I leave with a beard luxuriated. My unicorn companions have kept me away from all harm and danger. For I know with certainty and cataloguing that although bear, jackal, wolf, snake and leopard were my neighbours, upon crossing any of their paths they all but ignored me, as if I had ceased to be.

Now I am at sea and bound for my native France. How shall I present this tale of my time in India, and more precisely of my unicorn's? There are many more days before me to decide upon that course of action before setting foot ashore."

The End

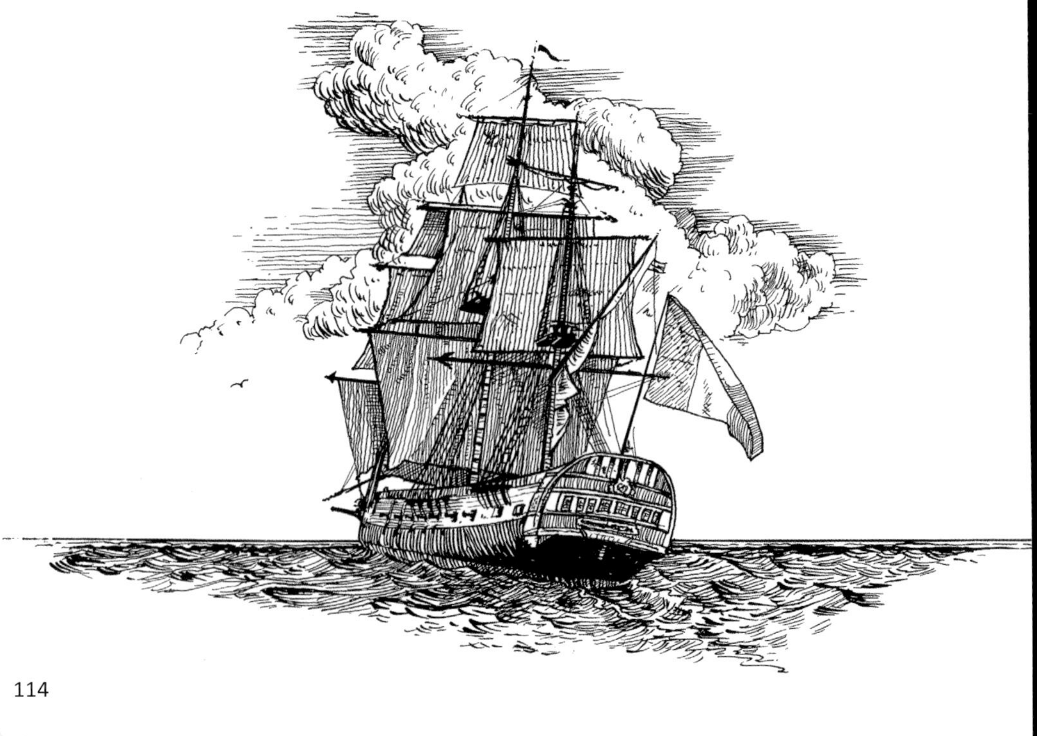

List of Paintings

Including the inspiration behind each one, by artist Anne Stokes

Inside front cover – Forest Maiden
A girl and her unicorn in the midst of a summer forest, bracken leaves swirling around them and butterflies floating in the air. A hint of a rainbow can be seen in the background.

Page 6/7 – Solace
This picture is about a bond of love and friendship between two beings. The forest is dark and foreboding. In contrast, the unicorn's white body and glowing horn shine out like a beacon of light to this melancholy lady. A heart pendant hangs from her hand suggesting a lost love for which her unicorn companion now provides comfort.

Page 25 – Moonlight Unicorn
I wanted to create a gothic style image with the unicorn appearing ghost-like before a cloudy moonlit sky and ruined castle. I found it interesting to use its reflection in the water to enhance the atmosphere and contrast the movement of the creature with the stillness of the water.

Page 28/29 – Pure Magic
A white creature against a snow covered forest was interesting to paint. The pose of the woman and the unicorn suggest that they have just met as she raises her hand to stroke its head in greeting. The snowy forest fades to purple shadows, a colour which is echoed in the purple of her robes.

Page 44 – Chase the Rainbow
I painted this picture some years ago as an image for a greetings card and as such it was designed to be an uplifting and attractive scene. I more recently added the rainbow effect for this book to fit with the text in the chapter. Sometimes it nice to revisit an older piece and add something new.

Page 41 – Forest Unicorn
My aim with this picture was to paint the unicorn in its natural forest environment. This painting was featured in Vanity Fair magazine and led to me, quite by coincidence, visiting their impressive offices in New York. A little unicorn magic at play there I'm sure.

Page 49 and the front cover – Blue Moon
The cover image and painting proven to be one of the most popular in this set. Maybe it's because it conveys an element of drama in the night setting and a fairy tale element with the characters. It was a great subject to paint and I enjoyed adding all the details of the forest and folds in the fabric. Did you spot the frog?

Page 50 – Everglade
The unicorn and the maiden is an enduring theme throughout history and one that I have used in a several pictures. Here the maiden holds a rose to symbolise purity and love, as she and the unicorn stand together under a Weeping Willow tree. There are many myths surrounding the power of the Willow and is use in magic and Celtic folklore.

Page 59 – Enlightenment
I wanted to feature a unicorn along side a heraldic representation and chose to do this using a stained glass window. Combining the magical light from the horn with the brightness shining through the glass suggested a sacred place that the unicorn has brought its magic to.

Page 65 – Journey's Start
The unicorn adopts a pose, pointing the way with front leg and horn, as the rider looks around as if taking in the task ahead. The light and her wand will guide them towards the right path on their journey.

Page 69 – Glimpse of a Unicorn
This was the first of the unicorn set that I painted. I wanted to convey the idea that the unicorn was appearing as if from a dream; a fleeting glimpse of magic. I used similar colours for the background and the creature, and a slightly blurred effect to blend them together and add a dream-like quality.

Page 75 – North Star
The North Star is one of the brightest stars in the sky, and here is lining up with the unicorn's horn and making the magical glow effect. The northern lights are seen in the sky also, which are a rare and magical event, a tie in with the rare and magical unicorn.

Page 79 – Winter Wonderland
A white unicorn in the white snow is a subject filled with symbolism of purity and mystery. I used blue tones in the shadows with a touch of pink in the

glow from the horn to emphasis magic there. Although there is beauty in snow, winter can be a cold and bleak time, and the unicorn appears as a blessing in this stark forest.

Page 82/83– Enchanted Pool
Despite a heady summer's day, the atmosphere by this forest pool is cool, as the enchantress is accompanied by her unicorn. A magical pentagram hangs from her hand on a thread of the unicorn's hair. They stand in unison, the contrast of their dark and light hair flowing together in the breeze.

Page 89 – Awake the Dawn
The black unicorn is a rare and magical beast. In this picture I portrayed it rearing up with a dramatic purple pink sky, as the black of night is broken and the dawn rises. The glow from the end of the horn indicates the magic that is in use as he brings forth the dawn light.

Page 91 – Realm of Darkness
A companion picture for Realm of Enchantment, but this one has a darker theme. A gothic styled sorceress rides her black winged unicorn accompanies by a small flying black dragon. They gallop across the picture to give an air of drama as they leave in haste.

Page 102/103 – Realm of Enchantment
This one arose from the challenge of combining three quintessential fantasy characters of a unicorn, a dragon and fairy in one picture. The solution was a fairy queen riding a unicorn steed with a small dragon on her arm, and all within an enchanted forest. A magical fairytale scene which I hoped would lead the viewer to think about these character and what might happen next.

Page 108/109 – Pure Heart
This picture was based on the classic legend of the maiden and the unicorn. My picture shows the close bond between them as they sit together, and the girl wears white symbolising her purity. There are two versions of this picture, a forest scene and this one with sunset lake in the background.

Page 118/119 – Beyond Words
A sculpture has been made from my Pure Heart artwork and seeing the back view of it inspired this picture. A view I perhaps would not have thought of without it. I enjoyed painting this version and as they sit looking out towards the far horizon together it seemed a perfect subject to finish the book with.

We have come to journeys end
In my embrace you shall slumber,
Dream, without fear my friend
We are and always will be together.

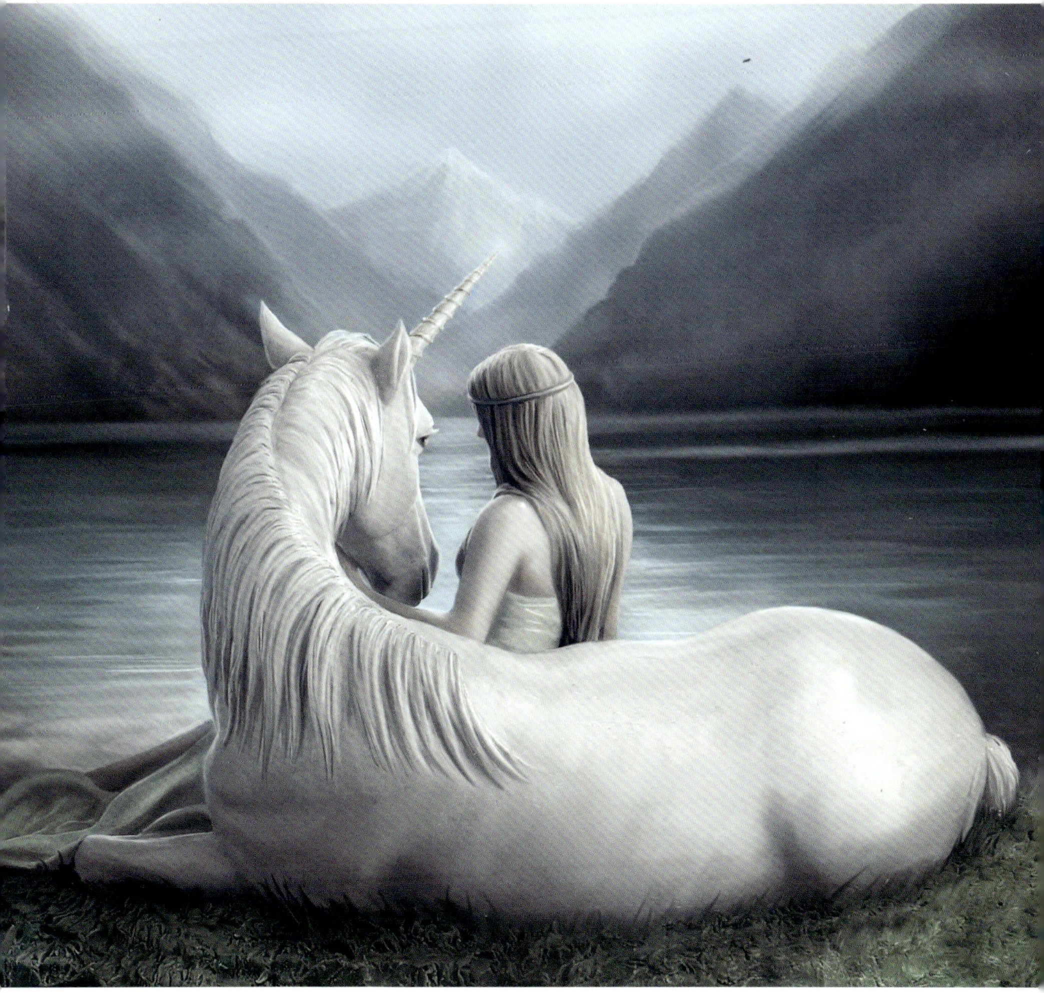

This book comes to its end, but the myth of the unicorn in all its forms will surely endure for many ages to come...

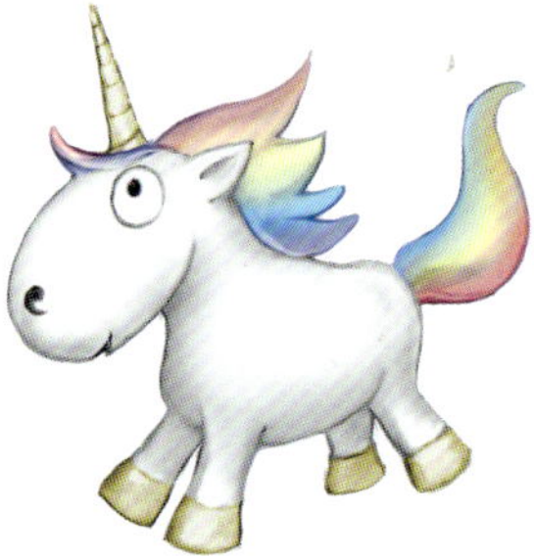